Domain Conditions in Social Choice Theory

Wulf Gaertner provides a comprehensive account of an important and complex issue within social choice theory: how to establish a social welfare function while restricting the spectrum of individual preferences in a sensible way. Gaertner's starting point is K. J. Arrow's famous 'Impossibility Theorem', which showed that no welfare function could exist if an unrestricted domain of preferences is to be satisfied, together with some other appealing conditions. A number of leading economists have tried to provide avenues out of this 'impossibility' by restricting the variety of preferences: here, Gaertner provides a clear and detailed account, using standardized mathematical notation, of well over 40 theorems associated with domain conditions.

Domain Conditions in Social Choice Theory will be an essential addition to the library of social choice theory for scholars and their advanced graduate students.

WULF GAERTNER is Professor of Economics at the University of Osnabrück. He has been a Visiting Scholar at Harvard University and at the London School of Economics and Political Science and has published extensively on social choice theory in leading journals. He is one of the managing editors of the journal *Social Choice and Welfare*.

Domain Conditions
in Social Choice Theory

Wulf Gaertner

University of Osnabrück

CAMBRIDGE
UNIVERSITY PRESS

CAMBRIDGE UNIVERSITY PRESS
Cambridge, New York, Melbourne, Madrid, Cape Town, Singapore, São Paulo

Cambridge University Press
The Edinburgh Building, Cambridge CB2 2RU, UK

Published in the United States of America by Cambridge University Press, New York

www.cambridge.org
Information on this title: www.cambridge.org/9780521791021

First published 2001
This digitally printed first paperback version 2006

A catalogue record for this publication is available from the British Library

Library of Congress Cataloguing in Publication data
Gaertner, Wulf.
Domain conditions in social choice theory / Wulf Gaertner.
p. cm.
Includes bibliographical references and index.
ISBN 0-521-79102-2
1. Social choice–Mathematical models.
2. Decision making–Mathematical models. I. Title
HB846.8.G34 2001
201′.13—dc21   2001025544

ISBN-13 978-0-521-79102-1 hardback
ISBN-10 0-521-79102-2 hardback

ISBN-13 978-0-521-02874-5 paperback
ISBN-10 0-521-02874-4 paperback

For Antje and Sabine

CONTENTS

Contents

Contents

PREFACE AND ACKNOWLEDGEMENTS

I am greatly indebted to Maurice Salles for kindly allowing me to use our joint article of 1981 as the basis for this monograph. My sincere thanks go to Amartya Sen both for numerous incisive comments and suggestions which he made on previous versions of the manuscript and for his continual encouragement. Extensive discussions, both orally and in written form, with Nick Baigent, Graciela Chichilnisky, Keith Dowding, Bill Gehrlein, Charles Horvath, Michel Le Breton, Andreu Mas-Colell, Eric Maskin, Iain McLean, John Weymark and Myrna Wooders are also gratefully acknowledged. Many thanks to Brigitte Arnold for patiently producing various versions of the manuscript. As a result of the hospitality of STICERD at the London School of Economics, the final revision could be prepared in a very stimulating and friendly environment. Last but not least, I wish to thank both Deutsche Forschungsgemeinschaft and Volkswagen-Stiftung for their generous financial support at various stages during my research.

Barbara Docherty, Chris Harrison and Michelle Williams of Cambridge University Press were very helpful during the production of this book.

CHAPTER 1

INTRODUCTION

The theory of social choice is abundant with impossibility theorems. The simplest impossibility result is probably the 'paradox of voting' which has been known for a long time. Imagine that there is a society comprising just three individuals who have to decide on whether to adopt policy x or policy y or policy z in order to increase economic welfare in their small community. Anticipating that their individual preferences will by no means be unanimous, the three members of society have agreed to use the simple majority decision rule as their method of aggregation. Let individual 1 prefer x to y, y to z and x to z, individual 2 prefer y to z, z to x and y to x, and individual 3 prefer z to x, x to y and z to y. Having applied the simple majority rule, the three persons obtain the following result: x is socially preferred to y, y to z and z to x. Obviously, each policy is dominated by one of the other two policies by a majority of two to one. What should be done in this situation? This is a difficult question indeed. The proposal to determine a sequence of pairwise decisions is no way out of the impasse, for the three individuals can be expected to disagree sharply on which pair of alternatives should be the first in the sequence of pairwise choices. Actually, in the latter part of the proof of his well-known impossibility result, Arrow (1951, 1963) used 'an appropriate adaptation of the paradox of voting' (1963, p. 100). Arrow's negative result is, of course, much more general than the cyclical structure of majority preference depicted above but with some justification perhaps, the paradox of voting can be described as the tip of an iceberg, the iceberg standing for a quite general axiomatic structure and its unviability.[1]

---

[1] As Sen (1985, p. 1769) writes, 'we must reject seeing the "Arrow problem" merely as a generalization of the paradox of voting. It is

According to McLean and London (1990), the roots of the theory of collective choice can be traced back to the end of the thirteenth century (possibly earlier than that[2]) when Ramon Lull designed two voting procedures that have a striking resemblance to what has 500 years later become known as the 'Borda method' and the 'Condorcet principle'. In his novel *Blanquerna* (around 1283) Lull made Natana explain a new electoral method to all the sisters in her nunnery, a method consisting of exhaustive pairwise comparisons, i.e., each candidate is compared to every other candidate under consideration. However, Natana (or Lull) does not advocate the choice of the 'Condorcet winner'[3] but the choice of the candidate who receives the highest number of votes in the aggregate of the pairwise comparisons. This procedure is identical to a method proposed by Borda in 1770 which, as was shown by Borda (1781) himself, must yield the same result as his well-known rank-order method.

The second procedure, devised in 1299, was put forward by Lull in his treatise *De Arte Eleccionis*. Here a successive voting rule is proposed that ends up with a 'Condorcet winner', if there exists one. Since not every logically possible pairwise comparison is made in determining the winner, the suggested procedure does not necessarily detect the existence of cycles. In the case that a cycle occurs, the outcome depends directly on the selected path of pairwise comparisons, but it is not clear whether Lull was aware of this fact.

---

much more than that.' On this and other paradoxes in economics, see De Marchi (1987).

[2] McLean and London refer to a letter by Pliny the Younger (around 90AD) in which secret ballots in the Roman Senate are discussed (see also Radice 1969, I, pp. 230–5). In that letter voting among three or more candidates is not mentioned. However, in a letter to Titius Aristo, voting over three distinct alternatives is discussed. Plinius describes a situation where one group of persons changes its preferences by dropping its preferred option, thereby generating an outcome that would not have been reached under pairwise majority decision over the original set of options (I owe this reference to Salvador Barberà).

[3] For chronological reasons, we have decided to put the concepts of Condorcet winner, Condorcet principle and Borda method in inverted commas here.

Nicolaus Cusanus had read *De Arte Eleccionis* (see Honecker 1937) but he rejected Lull's 'Condorcet procedure' and proposed instead a 'Borda rank-order method' with secret voting.[4] McLean and London indicate that Cusanus rejected Lull's 'Condorcet principle' for deeper reasons and not out of misunderstanding. In 1688 Pufendorf published his work *De jure naturae et gentium*, in which a few pages were devoted to various decision schemes such as majority and plurality rules.[5] Pufendorf, as well as Lull and Cusanus before him, explicitly mention the issue of telling the truth in an election.[6] The possibility of manipulation within collective choice processes is a phenomenon which has been receiving a lot of attention since the mid-1970s after the important findings of Gibbard (1973), Pattanaik (1973) and Satterthwaite (1973, 1975).

Much better known than Lull's, Cusanus' and Pufendorf's writings are the works by de Borda (1781) and the Marquis de Condorcet (1785). Condorcet extensively discussed the election of candidates under the majority rule. He was probably the first to demonstrate the existence of cyclical majorities for particular preference profiles (but nowhere did he discuss the symmetrical structure of our introductory example).[7] Condorcet called these situations 'contradictory', for in the case of three alternatives, let's say, any two of the propositions lead to

---

[4] See McLean and London (1990) for further references. Cusanus (1434) dealt with the election of a Holy Roman Emperor.

[5] For more details on Pufendorf's work see Lagerspetz (1986).

[6] Cusanus said in his *De concordantia catholica* (around 1434) that 'elections could be said to be disgracefully rigged by unjust pacts' (see McLean and London 1990).

[7] Though we have to concede that he was close to our 3×3 formulation, interestingly enough in the context of voting on economic policy: whether any restriction placed on commerce is an injustice or whether restrictions placed through general laws or by particular orders can be just (I am grateful to Emma Rothschild for this observation). According to Baker (1975), the paradoxical result of a voting cycle as in our introductory example was first properly called the 'Condorcet effect' by Guilbaud (1952).

a proposition which contradicts the third.[8] Condorcet proposed a resolution scheme for the case of cyclical majorities.[9] His arguments remained fragmentary, however, for the situation of more than three candidates.[10] Almost one hundred years later, Dodgson (1876) explicitly dealt with the case of cyclical majorities under various voting schemes but came to the conclusion that if there are persistent majority cycles there ought to be 'no Election' if this is an allowable outcome.[11]

To the best of our knowledge, none of the authors mentioned above wrote about a solution to the problem of cyclical majorities via restricting 'the shape'of individual preference orderings and 'the composition' of preference profiles.[12] Domain conditions of various forms for various collective choice rules are the topic of this monograph. In

[8] Black (1958, p. 167) finds Condorcet's use of the word 'contradictory' unfortunate. We fully agree with him when he writes that 'the danger is that describing these results as "contradictory" ... might suggest that the group has a scale of valuations which is the same in kind as that of the individual, which would be false: the individual values, the group does not; it reaches decisions through some procedure in voting'. On this point, see also De Marchi (1987) who claims that economists tend to employ 'micro-motives to account for aggregate relations whose entities they cannot explain'.

[9] Condorcet argued that in a case where, for example, a majority prefers x to y, y to z and z to x (as in our introductory example), the proposition with the smallest majority should be deleted and that alternative should be chosen which comes out as the winner under the two remaining propositions. Unfortunately, under the circumstances of our example above, Condorcet's suggestion would not help us to decide which of the three propositions we should delete.

[10] Part II of Black's book (1958) is an excellent source for further information on the history of the mathematical theory of collective decisions. See also Riker's (1986) historical remarks on weighted voting games.

[11] See Black (1958), pp. 224–34.

[12] Can one take the following quotations from Dodgson (see Black 1958, p. 225) as an indication that the author had a restriction on individual preferences in mind? 'When the issues to be further debated consist of, or have been reduced to, a single cycle, the Chairman shall inform the meeting how many alterations of votes each issue requires to give it a majority over every other separately ... If, when the majorities are found to be cyclical, any elector wishes to alter his paper, he may do so.'

his seminal work Arrow required that the range of the collective choice rule he was analysing (the social welfare function) be restricted to the set of orderings over the set of alternatives. One may find a lower degree of collective rationality quite acceptable. One can think of extending the range of the collective choice rule to include those social preference relations that are not orderings, but which always generate a nonempty choice set (the concept of a social decision function). Furthermore, Arrow and many other writers required the individual weak preference relations to be orderings, but one can think of arguments for weakening this condition and demand that the individual preference relations be reflexive, connected and quasi-transitive, not fully transitive. Both suggestions will be examined in detail. Furthermore we shall consider a variety of aggregation mechanisms, not only the simple majority decision rule but also – among others – special majority rules, multi-stage majority rules, simple games of various forms, social welfare functions and stable group decision functions.

The literature on domain conditions for collective choice rules can be split up into two large classes. The contributions to the first class study the aggregation problem for arbitrary finite sets of discrete alternatives. These options can be political parties or candidates representing these parties; these alternatives can also stand for particular economic and (or) social programmes. The contributions to the second class assume that the set of options has a topological structure. Most authors in this category suppose that the choice space is the n-dimensional Euclidean space. Within the first class, a further distinction can be made: The domain conditions with respect to the individual preference relations either have the characteristic of being exclusion conditions (particular individual preference relations are not permitted to be held by any member of society or particular preference relations are not allowed to occur in the presence of other preference relations), or the domain conditions admit all logically possible individual preference orderings, for example, but make certain requirements as to the distribution of individuals over these orderings.

The best-known example for the first type of restrictions is Black's (1948) condition of single-peaked preferences[13] which is depicted below in figure 1.1 for three alternatives x, y and z and three individuals. The vertical axis just indicates the order of preference – no cardinality is involved. We have chosen a particular ordering of the alternatives along the horizontal axis. However, there is flexibility with respect to the choice of this ordering. The lines between the symbols have no meaning. They simply help to interpret the structure of points as single-peaked.

As one can see from figure 1.1, a single-peaked graph is one which changes its direction at most once, when running from up to down. At an interpretative level, preferences are single-peaked if 'more' is strictly preferred to 'less' up to a point, and 'less' to 'more' beyond that point. Given a set of single-peaked curves, this restriction on preferences is rather easy to interpret. Let the committee's decision be with regard to the price of a new product. Each member of the committee will, in order to shape his (her) opinion on this matter, initially try to find

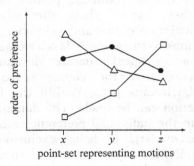

Figure 1.1.

[13] As a matter of fact, the idea of single-peakedness was developed independently by Arrow (though in print, Black was first). On this point, see the interview with K. J. Arrow by Kelly (1987).

out which is the optimal price for him (her). Once the optimal price has been fixed, 'the further any proposal departs from it on the one side or the other, the less he [she] will favour it' (Black, 1958, p. 9). Arrow (1951, 1963, p. 76) gives another example where Black's assumption seems to have been satisfied: the party structure of prewar European parliaments with a clear Left–Right ordering of the parties.

Let us take a second look at figure 1.1. One can easily see that alternative y lies between x and z in two of the three orderings and is 'best' in one ordering. Therefore, y is nowhere considered as 'the worst' of the three given options. This different, though an analytically equivalent aspect of single-peakedness, due to Sen (1966), uses a perspective which is quite different from the view on which Black and Arrow focused. This reinterpretation opened the door for various generalizations of the original condition which we shall discuss later on. Using Black's domain condition Arrow has shown that the simple majority decision rule generates a transitive social preference relation for any number of alternatives provided that the number of individuals is odd and the property of single-peakedness is fulfilled for every triple of alternatives.

The distributional requirements have been studied mainly for the method of majority decision. It is worth mentioning already at this point that there exists a logical relationship between some of the restrictions in this set of requirements and some of the exclusion conditions. Several of the authors in the area of distributional domain conditions have argued that the problem of the existence of a transitive social preference relation under the majority rule should be best studied for artificially constructed societies with so-called reduced preference profiles. The idea is as follows: Under the method of majority decision the two orderings 'x preferred to y and y preferred to z' and 'z preferred to y and y preferred to x' ($xPyPz$ and $zPyPx$, for short) cancel out as they are inverse to each other. Imagine that we have a society of six individuals with the following orderings: xP_1yP_1z, yP_2zP_2x, zP_3xP_3y, yP_4xP_4z, xP_5zP_5y, and zP_6yP_6x. Applying the majority rule we obtain the result that the society is indifferent among the three options. If we now add a seventh individual who has one of the six orderings above, this individual's ordering will determine the collective ordering. No majority cycle arises though, quite obviously, all the exclusion conditions are violated.

While the larger part of this monograph examines finite sets of discrete alternatives, the final chapter considers the aggregation issue for choice spaces with a topological structure. In various economic problems, the possible choices constitute a set of points in some appropriately defined multi-dimensional continuous choice space. For decisions on the composition of the federal budget, for example, or decisions on the production of various public goods the n-dimensional Euclidean space may be the appropriate space to consider. Another example would be choices over a set of social states that are characterized by numerical values only such as the unemployment rate, the inflation rate and the federal deficit, let's say. Individual preferences are represented by quasi-concave, differentiable utility functions defined over this space. Note that in those cases where the individual utility functions are defined on a compact interval of the real line, or where, for example, the north-east boundary of a feasible set is the focus of attention, as in many two-dimensional constrained maximization problems, quasi-concavity of the utility functions can be viewed as a generalization of Black's single-peakedness property. We shall discuss what impact the transition from finite sets of discrete alternatives to multi-dimensional topological spaces has on the issues of domain restriction and the existence of social choice rules. We also want to ask whether a logical relationship exists between the former, the standard approach so to speak, and the latter more recent method.

We should mention that Arrow chose a nontopological framework for his analysis and many papers that were written in response to his impossibility result did exactly the same. Continuity was not considered to be a relevant property. Of course, Arrow's impossibility result which we shall discuss briefly in chapter 2 can be formulated in n-dimensional continuous space and we would like to draw the reader's attention particularly to parts of chapter 4.1 and chapter 6.1 below (the reader may also wish to consult Inada 1964a for the existence resp. nonexistence of welfare functions in n-dimensional space). Note, for example, that spatial voting models, which we shall not discuss in this monograph, are often defined in two-dimensional Euclidean space. Both simple majority voting as an aggregation scheme and single-peakedness as a possible domain restriction are concepts that are directly applicable in such a space.

Is there any justification to consider domains that are restricted in the sense of not allowing particular individual preference relations to occur? We already mentioned that in the political arena a clear Left–Right ordering of the parties appears reasonable. If some individual is leaning toward the political Right, he or she will most probably prefer a candidate of this group to a candidate from the centre party and the latter most probably to a candidate from the left wing. Single-peakedness also makes good sense in various location problems when, for example, people want to live as close as possible to the city centre or students want to be as close as possible to the university campus.

In other instances, individuals wish to be as far as possible from a refuse disposal site or a coal-fired power station. Coming back to the Left–Right ordering of political parties, it is sometimes argued that people who tend to be extremists either vote for the extreme Right or the extreme Left, while they dislike parties in the middle of the spectrum. These cases are covered by so-called single-caved preferences, the mirror image of single-peakedness.

A common historical background or a common class background may bring about a fair amount of similarity among the individuals' preferences, and if a particular society consists mainly of two classes, the possibility that some preference relations will nowhere be encountered is relatively high. However, for a group of n individuals with $n - 1$ persons having single-peaked preferences and only one individual showing nonsingle-peaked preferences, cyclical majorities may arise. Therefore, a great deal of caution is advisable. On the other hand, Sen (1970, p. 165) is certainly right when he says that 'individual preferences are determined not by turning a roulette wheel over all possible alternatives'. Specific economic forces, education, but also, admittedly, manipulation are among those factors which can significantly shape individual preference relations. Therefore, in our opinion, it makes good sense to investigate the aggregation problem when only some, but not all logically possible individual preference relations occur.[14]

---

[14] A different perspective which, however, will not be followed in this monograph, was brought forward in an empirical investigation by Feld and Grofman (1987). They argued that requiring *each and every individual* in society to follow single-peakedness is demanding too much. What is sufficient for a transitive majority preference relation of the society as a whole is that *each subgroup* within society satisfy what they call the condition of ideologically ordered margins. The authors were investigating how individuals ranked the four Presidential candidates Carter, Kennedy, Ford and Reagan.

CHAPTER 2

NOTATION, DEFINITIONS AND TWO FUNDAMENTAL THEOREMS

The notation and definitions which we are introducing in this chapter will remain valid throughout chapters 2–5. Chapter 6 will use a somewhat different terminology.

Let $X = \{x,y,z,\ldots\}$ denote the set of all conceivable social states and let $N = \{1,\ldots,n\}$ denote a finite set of individuals or voters $(n \geq 2)$. Let R stand for a binary relation on X; R is a subset of ordered pairs in the product $X \times X$. We interpret R as a preference relation on X. Without any index, R refers to the social preference relation. When we speak of individual i's preference relation we simply write R_i. The fact that a pair (x, y) is an element of R will be denoted xRy; the negation of this fact will be denoted by $\neg xRy$. R is reflexive if for all $x \in X : xRx$. R is complete if for all $x,y \in X, x \neq y : xRy$ or yRx. R is said to be transitive if for all $x,y,z \in X : (xRy \wedge yRz) \rightarrow xRz$. The strict preference relation (the asymmetric part of R) will be denoted by $P : xPy \leftrightarrow [xRy \wedge \neg yRx]$. The indifference relation (the symmetric part of R) will be denoted by $I : xIy \leftrightarrow [xRy \wedge yRx]$. We shall call R a preference ordering (or an ordering or a complete preordering) on X if R is reflexive, complete and transitive. In this case, one obviously obtains for all $x,y \in X : xPy \leftrightarrow \neg yRx$ (reflexivity and completeness of R are sufficient for this result to hold), P is transitive and I is an equivalence relation; furthermore for all $x,y,z \in X : (xPy \wedge yRz) \rightarrow xPz$. R is said to be quasi-transitive if P is transitive. R is said to be acyclical if for all finite sequences $\{x_1,\ldots,x_k\}$ from X it is not the case that $x_1Px_2 \wedge x_2Px_3 \wedge \ldots \wedge x_{k-1}Px_k$ and x_kPx_1. The following implications clearly hold: R transitive $\rightarrow$ R quasi-transitive $\rightarrow$ R acyclical.

11

Domain conditions in social choice theory

An important result due to Sen (1970) states that if R is reflexive and complete, then a necessary and sufficient condition for the existence of a best element for all finite subsets S of X is that R be acyclical[1] (the existence of a best element for all S means that for each S, there exists $x \in S$ such that for all $y : y \in S \to xRy$). The interest in the property of acyclicity is due to the close relationship between this result and the existence of social decision functions.

In the context of social choice theory, the following interpretations can be attached to the relations R, P and I. xRy means that 'x is at least as good as y'; xPy means that 'x is better than y'; and xIy means that 'there is an indifference between x and y'.

Let A denote the set of preference relations on X, B denote the set of preference relations which are reflexive and complete on X, C denote the set of preference relations which are reflexive, complete and acyclical on X, D the set of preference relations which are reflexive, complete and quasi-transitive on X, and E the set of preference orderings on X. Obviously, $E \subset D \subset C \subset B \subset A$. $A', B', \ldots$ will stand for subsets of $A, B, \ldots$ fulfilling particular restrictions. A^n will denote the Cartesian product $A' \times \ldots \times A'$, n-times. An element of A^n is an n-tuple of preference relations $(R_1, \ldots, R_n)$ or the profile of an n-member society consisting of preference relations.

A collective choice rule is a mapping from A^n to A. A social welfare function is a mapping from E^n to E. A social welfare function for quasi-transitive individual preferences is a mapping from D^n to E. A social decision function of type QT is a mapping from E^n to D. A social decision function is a mapping from E^n to C. A social decision function is a collective choice rule such that a choice function is generated over the set of alternatives. We shall also consider social decision functions which are defined on D^n (see Arrow 1951, 1963; Fishburn 1970; Inada 1970; Sen 1970; Pattanaik 1971; Mas-Colell and Sonnenschein 1972).

---

[1] It may be of interest to compare this result with the one given by von Neumann and Morgenstern (1953, pp. 594–602). See also Pattanaik (1971) and Nakamura (1975).

In our introductory remarks, we have alluded to Arrow's famous impossibility theorem several times already. It is high time, therefore, that we give a brief account of his fundamental result. This result says that there does not exist a social welfare function if this mapping which we denote by $f(R_1, \ldots, R_n)$ is to satisfy the following four conditions:

Condition U (Unrestricted Domain). The domain of the mapping f includes all logically possible n-tuples of individual orderings on $X(\mathcal{E}' = \mathcal{E})$.

Condition P (Weak Pareto Principle). For any x,y in X, if everyone in society strictly prefers x to y, then xPy.

Condition I (Independence of Irrelevant Alternatives). If for two profiles of individual orderings $(R_1, \ldots, R_n)$ and $(R'_1, \ldots, R'_n)$, every individual in society has exactly the same preference with respect to any two alternatives x and y, then the social preference with respect to x and y must be the same for the two profiles. In other words, if for any pair x, y and for all i, xR_iy iff xR'_iy, and yR_ix iff yR'_ix, then $f(R_1, \ldots, R_n)$ and $f(R'_1, \ldots, R'_n)$ must order x and y in exactly the same way.

Condition D (Nondictatorship). There is no individual i in society such that for all profiles in the domain of f and for all pairs of alternatives x and y in X, if xP_iy, then xPy.

Theorem 1 (Arrow's General Possibility Theorem 1951, 1963). For a finite number of individuals and at least three distinct social alternatives, there is no social welfare function f satisfying conditions U, P, I and D.

For Arrow, these four conditions on f (or five conditions if the demand that the social preference relation be an ordering is counted as a separate requirement) were necessary requirements in the sense that 'taken together they express the doctrines of citizens' sovereignty and rationality in a very general form, with the citizens being allowed to have a wide range of values' (Arrow 1951, 1963, p. 31).

The second fundamental result refers to Gibbard and Satterthwaite. It is also a negative result in the sense that there exists no nonmanipulable or strategy-proof and nondictatorial voting procedure. Since precise definitions will be given in chapter 4, we shall be a bit loose here. A voting procedure is a mapping F which for each preference profile $(R_1, \ldots, R_n)$ and for each given non-empty set of alternatives S generates a unique social choice, i.e. a unique element from S. F is nonmanipulable if for no preference profile and for no given set of alternatives some individual can improve upon the social outcome relative to his or her truthful ordering by misrepresenting the true preferences.

Theorem 2 (Gibbard 1973; Satterthwaite 1975). Under the condition of unrestricted domain, every voting procedure with its range containing at least three outcomes is nonmanipulable or strategy-proof iff it is dictatorial.

We think that one can state without exaggeration that both impossibility theorems have become milestones, and not only in social choice theory proper. While the number of papers emanating from Arrow's result can be called uncountable if we use everyday language and not correct mathematical terminology (see Kelly's 1991 social choice bibliography and its updated 1998 version available on the internet), Moulin (1996) listed more than 180 papers on strategy-proofness.

We have already stated in our introduction that domain conditions of various forms for various collective choice mechanisms are the topic of this monograph. Clearly, by admitting only a proper subset of the set of all logically possible preference profiles, both Arrow's negative result and the impossibility result of Gibbard and Satterthwaite (as well as many other impossibility results in social choice theory) can be circumvented. There are, of course, various other ways to get around these impossibilities, and by no means do we want to claim that among all the possible escape routes, the domain-restriction variant is the most important path to follow.

Let us be a bit more specific before we continue with our main theme. Hansson (1973) stated that Arrow's impossibility theorem 'is really a theorem about the independence condition'. Indeed, this condition plays a crucial role in

Arrow's proof as well as in the proofs of many other Arrow-type impossibility results. Arrow himself said that 'social decision processes which are independent of irrelevant alternatives have a strong practical advantage' (1951, 1963, p. 110). What kind of aggregation rules do we get, once weakenings of Arrow's independence condition are permissible?

A prominent candidate along this line is the class of positionalist voting procedures. The Borda rule perhaps is the best-known scheme within this class where scores are attached to the positions of the alternatives in the individuals' orderings. In the Borda scheme, the scores or ranks decline when one goes from more preferred to less preferred alternatives, with a constant rank difference of '1' for any two adjacent positions. Clearly, the Borda voting rule (in its so-called 'broad version') only satisfies weakenings of Arrow's independence requirement. On the other hand, this method fulfils all the other Arrow axioms.

Another way to avoid Arrow's negative result would be to widen the informational framework by using utility information that is finer than that of purely ordinal preferences with no trace at all of any degree of interpersonal comparability. One could imagine turning to ordinal utilities with level-comparability among the individuals. One would, for example, want to know whether person 1 in state x is better or worse off than person 2 or person 3 in state y, let's say. The Rawlsian difference principle (Rawls 1971) focuses on the position of the worst-off (group of) individual(s) and looks for the policy alternative that maximizes the well-being of the worst-off. In this framework, we obtain what some have called a 'positional dictatorship'. There would also be the possibility to introduce cardinal utilities with the option to compare utility gains and losses among the members of society. The best-known modern version of utilitarian rules is the one proposed by Harsanyi (1955) which is based on the Bayesian concept of rationality. Both Harsanyi's approach and the axiomatized version of Rawls' lexicographic maximin principle satisfy nondictatorship, the Pareto principle and the independence condition, each of them appropriately reformulated within the respective informational framework (see, e.g., D'Aspremont and Gevers 1977). Last but not least in our enumeration, and somewhat further away from Arrow's axiomatic framework than the other approaches is the concept of fair allocations, a notion that goes back to Foley (1967) and Kolm (1971). Fair allocations are both Pareto-efficient and envy-free. This approach is embedded in the standard microeconomic framework with purely ordinal preferences and no trace at all of interpersonal comparability of utilities.

All these avenues – and several others – are worth pursuing in detail, but doing this would have meant writing a different monograph. Also, books of such a wide scope already exist in the social choice literature. On the other hand, not much has been written on the issue of domain restrictions and its many ramifications within collective choice theory.

CHAPTER 3

THE EXISTENCE OF COLLECTIVE CHOICE RULES UNDER EXCLUSION CONDITIONS FOR FINITE SETS OF DISCRETE ALTERNATIVES

In this chapter we study various weakenings of the condition of unrestricted domain. In other words, we are looking for restrictions on individual preferences such that social preference relations with varying degrees of rationality exist (transitive, quasi-transitive or acyclical). A common feature of these restrictions is that either certain individual preference relations are totally excluded or particular individual preference relations are not allowed to occur in the presence of other relations. We shall say that an exclusion condition is sufficient for the existence of a social welfare function, for example, if whenever $\mathcal{E}' \subset \mathcal{E}$ satisfies this condition for any N and any n-tuple $(R_1, \ldots, R_n)$, the generated social relation is an ordering. Furthermore, an exclusion condition is said to be necessary if for all N and all n-tuples $(R_1, \ldots, R_n)$ the social relation is an ordering only if $\mathcal{E}' \subset \mathcal{E}$ satisfies this condition. In other words, whenever $\mathcal{E}' \subset \mathcal{E}$ violates this condition, there is some set N and some n-tuple $(R_1, \ldots, R_n)$ such that the ordering property does not hold.[1] Inada (1969) emphasizes that the aim is to find maximal lists of individual orderings in the sense that any wider list may result in a violation of

---

[1] These are not the only possible definitions of a necessary and sufficient condition. For a justification of the concepts used here as well as alternative definitions see Sen and Pattanaik (1969); Pattanaik (1971); Fine (1973); Kelly (1974a); Kaneko (1975), and subsection 5.1.1 below. Kelly, for example, relates the concept of necessity in the sense of Inada, Sen and Pattanaik to cases of fixed numbers of voters.

the ordering property. These definitions of sufficiency and necessity are particularly useful in the present analysis where the aim is to find structural conditions on preferences (or particular patterns such as the one in our introduction) without considering numbers of voters and the distribution of voters over the set of individual preferences.

3.1 The method of majority decision

The first collective choice rule that was examined in the context of domain conditions was the method of simple majority decision.[2] It is a single-stage rule in the sense that just one majority voting operation is involved. We assume that the individual preference relations are reflexive and complete. We let $N(xR_iy)$ denote the number of individuals for whom xR_iy.

Definition. The method of majority decision is a collective choice rule defined on B'^n such that

$$\forall(R_1, \ldots, R_n),\ \forall x, y \in X : xRy \leftrightarrow [N(xR_iy) \geq N(yR_ix)].$$

Clearly, the range of this collective choice rule is the set B. Note that the definition just given is not the only one possible. Equivalent formulations are

$$\forall(R_1, \ldots, R_n),\ \forall x, y \in X : \quad xRy \leftrightarrow [N(xP_iy) \geq N(yP_ix)],$$
$$\forall(R_1, \ldots, R_n),\ \forall x,, y \in X : \quad xPy \leftrightarrow [N(xR_iy) > N(yR_ix)],$$
$$\text{and}\quad yRx \quad \text{otherwise,}$$
$$\forall(R_1, \ldots, R_n),\ \forall x, y \in X : \quad xPy \leftrightarrow [N(xP_iy) > N(yP_ix)],$$
$$\text{and}\quad yRx \quad \text{otherwise.}$$

---

[2] See Black (1948). A complete characterization of the majority rule was given by May (1952).

3.1.1 The case where the individual preferences are orderings

3.1.1.1 The method of majority decision is a social welfare function

In the following we shall characterize the sets $\mathcal{E}'$ for which the method of majority decision generates a transitive social relation. Since the transitivity property is a condition which is defined over triples, we can state the relevant conditions in terms of triples of distinct alternatives (x,y,z); a, b and c are three distinct variables, each of which can assume one of the values x, y and z. Before we introduce various restrictions, we wish to separate out those individuals who are indifferent among all the alternatives (the so-called unconcerned individuals). A concerned individual for a set of options is then one who is not indifferent between every pair of elements.

Definition. Extremal Restriction ER (Sen and Pattanaik 1969). $\forall a, \forall b, \forall c$:

$$[\exists i : aP_ib \wedge bP_ic \rightarrow \forall j : (cP_ja \rightarrow cP_jb \wedge bP_ja)].$$

If for some R_i, a is preferred to b, and b is preferred to c, then for all R_j such that c is preferred to a, c is also preferred to b and b is preferred to a. In other words, if there is some individual with a strong ordering over the triple (a,b,c) and if there are other individuals who regard as uniquely best the alternative the first person regards as uniquely worst, then the other persons regard as uniquely worst the alternative which the first individual regards as best. It is in this sense that we can speak of an extremal restriction.

It is not difficult to show that this condition is equivalent to the union of three restrictions proposed by Inada (1964b, 1969): 'antagonistic' preferences, 'echoic' preferences, and 'dichotomous' preferences.[3] Dichotomous preferences, for example, are given if within a triple there is at least one pair of alternatives between which each

---

[3] See subsection 3.1.2.1 below.

Domain conditions in social choice theory

individual is indifferent (the pair need not be the same for different individuals). Condition *ER* satisfies this property trivially.

Theorem 3 (Inada 1969; Sen and Pattanaik 1969). Iff the set of individual orderings $\mathcal{E}'$ satisfies condition *ER* for every triple of alternatives, the method of majority decision is a social welfare function.

Condition *ER* is unique in the sense that when the simple majority rule is the underlying mechanism, it is the only condition which proves to be necessary and sufficient for the existence of a social welfare function. Since Black's investigations, on single-peaked preferences in particular, we know that there are other restriction conditions which generate a social welfare function. For these conditions, an additional requirement has to be made (an assumption, however, which cannot be easily justified): The number of concerned voters has to be odd.

Definition. Value Restriction *VR* (Sen 1966).[4]
$\exists a, \exists b, \exists c$ such that for all R_i concerned:

$$[\forall i : aP_ib \vee aP_ic] \vee [\forall i : bP_ia \vee cP_ia]$$
$$\vee[\forall i : (aP_ib \wedge aP_ic) \vee (bP_ia \wedge cP_ia)].$$

In the triple (x,y,z) there is an option a such that all concerned individuals agree that it is not worst, or agree that it is not best, or agree that it is not medium.

The property of value restriction generalizes various conditions proposed by Black (1948, 1958); Coombs (1954, 1964); Vickrey (1960); Arrow (1963, chap. 7); Inada (1964b); Ward (1965).[5]

The next condition is a weaker version of Inada's (1969) restriction of 'taboo preferences'.

---

[4] See also Majumdar (1969).

[5] The notion of single-peakedness which Arrow introduced was more general than Black's original version. See, however, Black (1958, chap. 5). See also Fishburn (1972a, 1973). Arrow and Raynaud (1986) discuss two conditions by Romero (1978), called 'arboricity' and 'quasi–unimodality', that lend themselves to meaningful interpretations but do not go beyond single-peakedness.

Definition. Limited Agreement LA (Sen and Pattanaik 1969). $\exists a, \exists b : [\forall i : aR_ib]$.

In the triple (x,y,z) there is an ordered pair (a,b) such that every individual regards a to be at least as good as b.

Sen (1970) has shown that conditions ER, VR and LA are completely independent of each other, i.e. any pair of these three could be satisfied without the third, and any one of these could be fulfilled without the other two. The following profile, for example, satisfies condition ER, but VR and LA are not satisfied:

$$xP_1yP_1z$$
$$zP_2yP_2x$$
$$yP_3xI_3z$$
$$xI_4zP_4y.$$

Two strict orderings over a triple always satisfy VR. In the following profile LA is also fulfilled whereas ER is not:

$$xP_1yP_1z$$
$$zP_2xP_2y.$$

In the last profile presented here, ER and LA are both satisfied but VR is not:

$$xP_1yP_1z$$
$$yP_2zI_2x$$
$$zI_3xP_3y.$$

Theorem 4 (Inada 1969). Iff the set of individual orderings $\mathcal{E}'$ satisfies for every triple of alternatives at least one of the conditions ER, VR and LA, the method of majority decision is a social welfare function, provided the number of concerned voters is odd.

If the oddness requirement appears unacceptable and the condition ER somewhat difficult to interpret, one can decide to be less demanding and resort to the concept of a social decision function which requires the existence of best elements, not complete orderings. The existence of a best element guarantees that there is a Condorcet winner.

3.1.1.2 The method of majority decision is a social decision function

We now characterize the sets of individual preference orderings $\mathcal{E}'$ for which the method of majority decision generates social preference relations which lie in $\mathcal{C}$.

Theorem 5 (Sen and Pattanaik 1969). Iff the set of individual orderings $\mathcal{E}'$ satisfies at least one of the conditions ER, VR and LA for every triple of alternatives, the method of majority decision is a social decision function.

Consider the following profile that satisfies neither ER, nor VR, nor LA:

$$xP_1yP_1z$$
$$yI_2zP_2x$$
$$zP_3xI_3y.$$

If each of the three orderings is held by exactly one person, quasi-transitivity is satisfied under the method of majority decision. If two persons have P_1 and one person each holds the second and the third ordering, quasi-transitivity is no longer satisfied, but acyclicity is. In both cases, a social decision function exists. If three individuals have P_1, two persons hold the second ordering and two persons have the third ordering, we obtain a strict preference cycle under the simple majority rule. These cases nicely illustrate the concept of necessity that we introduced at the beginning of this chapter.

Note that the antecedent in theorem 5 is identical to the one in theorem 4 except for the suppression of the oddness requirement. We should like to mention in passing that in the sufficiency part of the proof it is shown that the method of majority decision is a social decision function of type QT. For finite X, the theorem implies that for all $S \subset X$ there exists $x \in S$ such that xRy for all $y \in S$.[6]

---

[6] For finite X, there exists a best alternative for the entire set under the method of majority decision if every triple of Pareto-optimal alternatives in the set satisfies ER or VR (Sen and Pattanaik 1969).

3.1.1.3 The method of majority decision and order restricted preferences

Rothstein (1990) has proposed looking at a given set of individual orderings in a somewhat different way. According to him, individual preferences are order restricted on $S \subset X$ if there is a renumbering of the individuals such that for each distinct pair of alternatives (say x and y), all those persons who strictly prefer x to y are numbered lower than all those who are indifferent between the two, and these again are numbered lower than all those who strictly prefer y to x (or conversely). This means that for each distinct pair of alternatives, the individuals are partitioned into three groups. Any of these groups may be null, of course.

Rothstein shows that order restriction on triples is strictly stronger than value restriction but strictly weaker than single-peakedness and its symmetric counterpart single-cavedness. It is clear that the following result holds true.

Theorem 6 (Rothstein 1990). If the set of individual orderings $\mathcal{E}'$ satisfies order restriction for every triple of alternatives, the method of majority decision yields a relation R that generates a nonempty choice set for every finite set $S \subset X$.

Rothstein claims that his condition proves particularly useful in models where there is a natural ordering of the voters. The author argues that in a vote over alternative tax and transfer schemes it is more suitable to work with an ordering of the individuals than with a structuring of the alternatives.[7]

---

[7] Rothstein shows that Roberts' (1977) property of hierarchical adherence is a case of order restricted preferences (see also Hamada 1973). A similar approach has been taken by Gans and Smart (1996) whose condition of single-crossing preferences is equivalent to Rothstein's requirement. Gans and Smart also argue in favour of an ordering of the voters and emphasize the ease with which their condition can be checked in applications. One of their examples is a vote of labour union members over alternative employment–wage combinations.

3.1.2 *The case where the individual preferences are quasi-transitive*

3.1.2.1 The method of majority decision is a social welfare function for quasi-transitive individual preferences

For the results that follow some of the conditions which were presented in subsection 3.1.1 have to be modified.

Definition. Generalized Value Restriction VR^* (Fishburn 1970).
In the triple (x,y,z) there exists an element, say a, such that for $b \neq a, c \neq a(b \neq c)$ in (x,y,z)

$$(aP_ib \vee aP_ic) \quad \text{for all} \quad R_i \quad \text{concerned,}$$
$$\vee(bP_ia \vee cP_ia) \quad \text{for all} \quad R_i \quad \text{concerned,}$$
$$\vee[(aP_ib \wedge aP_ic) \vee (bP_ia \wedge cP_ia)$$
$$\vee(aI_ib \wedge aI_ic)] \quad \text{for all} \quad R_i.$$

It is clear that if every R_i is an ordering, then VR^* is equivalent to VR (the individuals with $aI_ib \wedge aI_ic$ in the definition above would then automatically become unconcerned). If, however, every R_i is reflexive, complete, and quasi-transitive, then VR^* is weaker then VR. For example (Pattanaik 1970a), if $(xP_iy \wedge yI_iz \wedge zI_ix)$ for some individuals and $(yP_ix \wedge yI_iz \wedge zI_ix)$ for the others, then VR^* is satisfied though VR is not.

Definition. Generalized Limited Agreement LA^* (Inada 1970).
In the triple (x,y,z) there exists some ordered pair, say (a,b), such that for all $i \in \{1,\ldots,n\}$,

> if R_i is transitive, then aR_ib;
>
> if R_i is not transitive, then aP_ib.

Again, if every R_i is an ordering, LA^* is equivalent to LA.

Definition. Dichotomous Preferences DP (Inada 1969).
For all $i \in \{1,\ldots,n\}, R_i$ is transitive and for some distinct a,b in $(x,y,z) : aI_ib$.

Definition. Antagonistic Preferences AP (Inada 1969).
For all $i \in \{1, \ldots, n\}, R_i$ is transitive and there exists an ordered triple (a,b,c) such that for some $j,k \in \{1, \ldots, n\}, aP_jbP_jc$ and cP_kbP_ka and for all i distinct from j and k, aI_ic.

Definition. Strict Agreement SA (Pattanaik and Sengupta 1974).
There are three distinct alternatives a,b,c in (x,y,z) such that one of the following three cases holds:

(i) for all $i \in \{1, \ldots, n\}$, if R_i is concerned and transitive on (x,y,z), then $aP_ic \wedge bP_ic$, and if R_i is not transitive on (x,y,z), then $aR_ic \wedge bR_ic$;

(ii) for all $i \in \{1, \ldots, n\}$, if R_i is concerned and transitive on (x,y,z), then $aP_ib \wedge aP_ic$, and if R_i is not transitive on (x,y,z), then $aR_ib \wedge aR_ic$;

(iii) for all $i \in \{1, \ldots, n\}$, if R_i is concerned and transitive on (x,y,z), then $aP_ic \wedge (aP_ib \vee bP_ic)$, and if R_i is not transitive on (x,y,z), then $aR_ib \wedge bR_ic \wedge aR_ic$.

The following theorem, which was formulated by Fishburn (1972b) and, independently, by Pattanaik and Sengupta (1974), characterizes the sets of preference relations $\mathcal{D}'$ which guarantee that the social relation is an ordering generated by the method of majority decision.

Theorem 7 (Fishburn 1972b; Pattanaik and Sengupta 1974). Iff the set of individual relations $\mathcal{D}'$ satisfies one of the conditions VR^*, LA^*, DP, AP and SA for every triple of alternatives, the method of majority decision is a social welfare function for quasi-transitive individual preferences, provided the number of concerned individuals with a transitive preference relation R_i is odd.[8]

This result is a generalization of theorem 4 above. It is of particular interest if there are reasons to believe that individual preferences are likely to be quasi-transitive

---

[8] Gaertner and Salles (1981) have used condition ER instead of conditions DP and AP when stating this theorem (see also Inada 1970, p. 31 on this point).

rather than transitive. Weinstein (1968) argues that there are situations when an individual cannot distinguish perfectly between two alternatives because these objects are less than one 'just noticeable difference' apart. In such cases, it may happen that the individual is indifferent between x and y, and also between y and z, but that the difference between x and z is large enough to be discernible so that x is preferred to z. Thus, intransitivity of the indifference relation may arise.[9] Weinstein argues that what determines the range of the just noticeable difference is the comparability of the alternatives. While quantities of money are easily comparable, this may no longer be the case when choices are made between commodity bundles. Comparability seems to decrease with an increase in the complexity of the objects of choice.

3.1.2.2 The method of majority decision is a social decision function of type QT for quasi-transitive individual preferences

We are now interested in a characterization of the sets $\mathcal{D}'$ such that a quasi-transitive social preference relation exists.

Theorem 8 (Fishburn 1970; Inada 1970[10]). Iff the set of individual preference relations $\mathcal{D}'$ satisfies at least one of the conditions VR^*, LA^*, DP and AP for every triple of alternatives, the method of majority decision is a social decision function of type QT for quasi-transitive individual preferences.[11]

Sen and Pattanaik (1969) showed in the necessity part of their proof of theorem 5 above that whenever a violation of the relevant restrictions led to a violation of quasi-transitivity of the social preference relation, acyclicity did not hold either. That this fact does not carry over to the present case of quasi-transitive individual preferences

---

[9] See also Armstrong (1951) and Inada (1970) on this point.
[10] For a correction of Inada's proof see Salles (1974).
[11] In relation to this result see also Jain (1986a) and the end of section 3.2 below.

was demonstrated by Inada (1970, p. 39) by means of the following simple example.

Let the list of individual preferences be as follows. There are n_1 individuals who have $zI_1xP_1yI_1z$ and n_2 individuals having $xI_2yP_2zI_2x$. If $n_1 > 0$ and $n_2 > 0$, we obtain xPy, yPz and zIx. Thus, quasi-transitivity of the social relation is violated but there is no violation of acyclicity.

3.2 Alternative single-stage social decision rules

In this section we wish to look at collective choice rules other than the method of simple majority decision. We shall in particular consider the strict majority rule, the semi-strict majority rule, and a class of special majority rules.[12]

Sen and Pattanaik (1969) have shown that if a binary collective choice rule is neutral and nonnegatively responsive,[13] then a quasi-transitive social preference relation will be generated if the individual orderings are value restricted for every triple of alternatives. An example of a collective choice rule that is neutral, anonymous and nonnegatively responsive is the strict majority rule.[14]

Definition. The Strict Majority Rule. $\forall(R_1, \ldots, R_n)$, $\forall x, y \in X : xPy \leftrightarrow N(xP_iy) > \frac{1}{2} \cdot |N|$, where $|N|$ is the total number of individuals. Further, $xRy \leftrightarrow \neg yPx$.

Starting from this definition, one can now define a continuum of collective choice rules that will lie between the strict majority rule and the method of simple majority decision. Let N^* be the number of nonindifferent individuals in the relation between two distinct alternatives x and y.

---

[12] The strict majority rule corresponds to the method of nonminority decision in Pattanaik (1971, chap. 6). See also Dummett and Farquharson (1961), Fine (1973) and section 3.5 below.

[13] For a definition of these properties, see Sen (1970, chap. 5).

[14] The simple majority rule is neutral, anonymous and positively responsive (May 1952).

Domain conditions in social choice theory

Definition. The Semi-Strict Majority Rule. $\forall(R_1, \ldots, R_n)$, $\forall x,y \in X : xPy \leftrightarrow N(xP_iy) > \frac{1}{2}[p \cdot |N| + (1-p)N^*]$, for some given p chosen from the open interval $]0, 1[$. Further, $xRy \leftrightarrow \neg yPx$.

If $p = 0$ we obviously obtain the simple majority rule, for $p = 1$ we have the strict majority rule. We know that if every individual has dichotomous preferences, the simple majority rule generates a quasi-transitive (even fully transitive) social preference relation. The strict majority rule also yields a quasi-transitive social relation under condition DP. However, for no $p \in]0, 1[$ does the semi-strict majority rule generate a quasi-transitive social relation for dichotomous preferences of the individuals (Jain 1986b). As for condition ER, we have seen that it is a (necessary and) sufficient condition for the existence of a transitive social relation under the simple majority rule. Extremal restriction is no longer sufficient even for quasi-transitivity if we apply the strict majority rule or the semi-strict majority rule. Considering the continuous variation of p in the open interval $]0, 1[$ we, therefore, observe some sort of discontinuity, for with p appropriately chosen we can come arbitrarily close to the points $p = 0$ and $p = 1$.

Jain (1986b) has shown that a necessary and sufficient condition for quasi-transitivity of the social preference relation under every semi-strict majority rule is that condition VR or the condition of absence of a unique extremal value holds for every triple of alternatives. Furthermore, a necessary and sufficient condition for transitivity of the social relation under every semi-strict majority rule is that the condition of strongly antagonistic preferences or partial agreement or strict placement restriction[15] holds over every triple of alternatives.

---

[15] For the sake of brevity, we abstain from stating the exact definitions of most of the restriction conditions. After the detailed analysis in the preceding sections the reader will guess their meanings with some degree of accuracy at least. However, the strict placement restriction should be explained. This condition is satisfied over a triple if there exists (i) an alternative which is uniquely best in every concerned R_i, or (ii) an alternative which is uniquely worst in every concerned R_i, or

We now wish to consider a class of special majority rules. A special majority rule belonging to this class requires that an alternative x be declared socially preferred to another alternative y iff the number of individuals who prefer x to y is greater than $p\,(\frac{1}{2} < p < 1)$ of the total of those who have strict preferences between x and y. Those who are indifferent between two alternatives are not taken into account. This is a characteristic which is also satisfied by the simple majority rule. The strict and semi-strict majority rules, on the other hand, take those voters who are indifferent between two alternatives into consideration as we have seen above.

Definition. Special Majority Rules. $\forall(R_1, \ldots, R_n)$, $\forall x, y \in X : xRy \leftrightarrow \neg[N(yP_ix) > p \cdot [N(xP_iy) + N(yP_ix)]]$, where p is a fraction such that $\frac{1}{2} < p < 1$.

Jain (1983) has shown that for the case where the individual preference relations are orderings, the necessary and sufficient conditions for quasi-transitivity under the special majority rules are identical to the necessary and sufficient conditions for quasi-transitivity under the simple majority rule. This result, however, does not carry over to the case of full transitivity. Here, a condition called strong value restriction is necessary and sufficient for transitivity under all special majority rules, and this requirement is stronger than condition *ER*. How do the domain conditions for special majority rules look when the social preference relation is to satisfy quasi-transitivity and the individual preferences are quasi-transitive?

We say that in the triple (x,y,z) alternative x is proper best for individual i iff $(xP_iy \wedge xR_iz) \vee (xR_iy \wedge xP_iz)$, proper medium iff $(yP_ix \wedge xR_iz) \vee (yR_ix \wedge xP_iz) \vee (zP_ix \wedge xR_iy) \vee (zR_ix \wedge xP_iy)$ and proper worst iff $(yP_ix \wedge zR_ix) \vee (yR_ix \wedge zP_ix)$. Alternative x is said to be best, medium and worst, respectively, if in the above definitions all instances of a strict relation P_i are replaced by R_i.

(iii) an alternative which is uniquely medium in every concerned R_i, or
(iv) a pair of distinct alternatives such that every individual is indifferent between the elements of the pair.

Domain conditions in social choice theory

Definition. Strict Latin Square *SLS* (Jain 1986a).

$\{R_i, R_j, R_k\}$ form a strict Latin Square over a triple (x,y,z) iff there exist distinct a,b,c in (x,y,z) such that in R_i, a is best, b proper medium and c worst; in R_j, b is best, c proper medium and a worst, and in R_k, c is best, a proper medium and b worst.

This strict Latin Square will be denoted by $SLS(abca)$. Over a triple (x,y,z) there are two logically possible strict Latin Squares: $SLS(xyzx)$ and $SLS(xzyx)$. The set of all logically possible quasi-transitive R_i of $SLS(xyzx)$ will be denoted by $T(xyzx)$ and the set of all logically possible quasi-transitive R_i of $SLS(xzyx)$ by $T(xzyx)$.

Definition. Strict Latin Square Partial Agreement *SLSPA* (Jain 1986a).

A set $\mathcal{D}'$ of preference relations R_i satisfies *SLSPA* over the triple (x,y,z) iff the following holds: If there exists a strict Latin Square over (x,y,z), say $SLS(xyzx)$, involving a strong ordering or not fully transitive R_i (intransitive indifference I_i), then there exist distinct a, b in (x,y,z) such that $\forall R_i \in \mathcal{D}' \cap T(xyzx): aR_ib$ and for all intransitive I_i such that $I_i \in \mathcal{D}' \cap T(xyzx): aP_ib$.

We now obtain a necessary and sufficient condition for quasi-transitivity under the class of special majority rules.[16]

Theorem 9 (Jain 1986a). Let p be any number from the open interval $]\frac{1}{2}, 1[$ and let h be the special majority rule associated with p. Iff the set of individual preference relations $\mathcal{D}'$ satisfies condition *SLSPA* for every triple of alternatives, the special majority rule h generates a quasi-transitive social preference relation.

Jain mentions that the proof of his theorem is also valid for $p = \frac{1}{2}$. This implies that condition *SLSPA* is necessary

---

[16] Jain (1987) has also established a necessary and sufficient condition for quasi-transitivity under nonminority rules, when the individual preferences are quasi-transitive. The restriction on preferences is the strict Latin Square unique value restriction. We again abstain from giving further details.

and sufficient for quasi-transitivity under the simple majority rule. Therefore, by putting $p = \frac{1}{2}$, one obtains an alternative proof of theorem 8. In view of the Inada–Fishburn result, it follows that condition $SLSPA$ is logically equivalent to the union of conditions VR^*, LA^*, DP and AP.

3.3 Multi-stage majority decision rules

A multi-stage majority decision rule (some authors prefer to call it a representative majority group decision function) is a collective choice rule which is composed of a hierarchy of one or more majority voting operations in each of which the entries consist of individual weak preference relations or the results of majority voting operations which have already been performed at a lower level. For this class of group decision rules it is possible that the preference relation of individual k, let's say, enters into more than one majority voting operation. It can also enter more than once into one majority voting operation.[17]

The method of majority decision is a special element in this class of social decision rules in so far as it involves one and only one majority voting operation in which the preference relation of each individual enters exactly once.

A majority voting operation at the lowest level is an operation of order zero where each entry is an individual weak preference relation. A majority voting operation of order one is characterized by the fact that at least one entry is the value of a majority voting operation of order zero. More generally, a majority voting operation of order n is one in which each element is the value of a majority voting operation of order $n - 1$, or $n - 2$ or, ..., or zero, and at least one of these entries is the value of a majority voting operation of order $n - 1$.

Let us consider an example to clarify the multi-stage decision procedure. Suppose we have four individual order-

---

[17] This means that the possibility of a dictator in Arrow's (1951, 1963) sense is not excluded. See Batra and Pattanaik (1972a, n. 8).

ings R_1, R_2, R_3, R_4 and the following multi-stage majority decision rule:

$$((R_1, R_2), R_2, (R_2, R_3), R_4, R_4) =$$
$$((xP_1yP_1z, xP_2zP_2y), xP_2zP_2y,$$
$$(xP_2zP_2y, zP_3xP_3y), zP_4yP_4x, zP_4yP_4x).^{18}$$

Each of the majority voting operations (R_1, R_2) and (R_2, R_3) is a majority voting operation of order zero. The simple majority decision rule yields $(xPy \land xPz \land yIz)$ and $(xIz \land xPy \land zPy)$, respectively. The majority voting operation of order one (the highest order in our example) considers the outcome of the two majority voting operations of order zero together with the individual orderings R_2 and R_4, where the latter counts twice. The result of this order-one operation is $(xIz \land xPy \land zPy)$.

One should mention that given a finite sequence of individual preference relations, there are many different multi-stage majority decision rules. For the individual relations R_1, R_2, R_3 one can, for example, have $((R_1, R_3), R_2)$ or $((R_1, R_1, R_2, R_3), R_2, (R_1, R_3, (R_2, R_3)))$. For any particular rule, however, the structure of majority voting operations is the same for all pairs of alternatives.

For the case of only two alternatives, Murakami (1966, 1968), Fishburn (1971, 1974, 1975) and Fine (1972)[19] have presented alternative sets of conditions to characterize representative systems.[20] Fine, for example, has shown that strong monotonicity and self-duality are sufficient conditions for a social decision rule to be a representative system, and that monotonicity, self-duality and not being 'zigzag' are necessary and sufficient conditions. While self-duality means that the social decision rule treats alternatives equally or neutrally, the property of not

---

[18] xP_1yP_1z is short for $(xP_1y \land yP_1z \land xP_1z)$ and, analogously, for the other orderings.

[19] See also Fishburn (1979).

[20] For Murakami and Fishburn the term 'representative system' implies that it is a nondictatorial representative majority group decision function (see n. 17 above).

being 'zigzag' disallows the rule to preserve social indifference when there is a substantial fluctuation of individuals' preferences.

3.3.1 The case where the individual preferences are orderings

Value restriction, limited agreement and the oddness requirement are the essential characteristics in the following possibility result.

Theorem 10 (Batra and Pattanaik 1971). If a finite sequence of individual orderings satisfies *VR* or *LA* over every triple of alternatives, any multi-stage majority decision rule generates a social preference ordering, given that the number of entries concerned with respect to any triple of alternatives is odd for every majority voting operation involved.

The requirement that the number of entries concerned with respect to any triple be odd for every majority voting operation is indispensable.[21] Otherwise, the above theorem may not hold even if the number of concerned individuals is odd for every triple.[22] This can be easily seen from the following example given by the authors. Let the multistage majority decision rule be $((R_1,R_2),R_3) = ((xI_1yP_1z, xP_2yI_2z),yP_3zP_3x)$. Condition *VR* is clearly satisfied (z is not best); also the number of concerned voters is odd for the given triple. The majority voting operation of order zero yields $xPy \wedge xPz \wedge yPz$. However, the voting

---

[21] Since the method of majority decision is a special element of the present class of collective decision rules, as mentioned above, the reader should compare theorem 10 with theorems 3 and 4. Obviously, for the present class of rules, there is no domain condition which can do without the oddness requirement.

[22] Batra and Pattanaik (1971) have also considered the class of binary, decisive, neutral (dual) and strongly monotonic group decision rules (every multi-stage majority decision rule is binary, decisive, neutral and monotonic, but not necessarily strongly monotonic).

operation of order 1 yields an intransitive relation, viz.
$xIy \land yPz \land xIz$.

3.3.2 The case where the individual preferences
are quasi-transitive

In this case the oddness requirement is less stringent; it is
demanded only that the number of transitive and concerned entries in the final majority voting operation be
odd.

Theorem 11 (Batra and Pattanaik 1972a). Any multi-stage
majority decision rule generates a social preference ordering over the triple (x, y, z) if the finite sequence of individual preference relations from set $\mathcal{D}'$ satisfies condition
VR^* or condition LA^* over (x,y,z) and the number of entries
in the final majority voting operation which are concerned
with respect to (x,y,z) and transitive over it, is odd.

Theorem 11 may be considered as a generalization of
theorem 10. The rationality assumption with respect to
individual preferences has been weakened to quasi-transitivity and also the restriction on the number of voters is
less severe.[23]

3.4 The likelihood of no majority winner

Condorcet's paradox of voting occurs when each alternative in a voting process can be beaten by some other
alternative on the basis of the simple majority decision
rule. Imagine that there are three alternatives, three voters,
and only strict individual orderings are admitted. We then
have six logically possible strict orderings and arrive at
$6 \times 6 \times 6 = 216$ logically possible preference profiles for
the three-member society. For this simple case one can
easily see that 12 profiles out of the 216 situations give
rise to a majority cycle. If we make the assumption that
every individual ordering is as likely as every other (several

---

[23] The reader should also compare theorem 11 with theorem 7 above.

authors in this area of research call this assumption the 'impartial culture condition'), we see that a preference cycle occurs with a probability of 0.0555. How does this probability change when we increase the number of options or (and) increase the number of voters? Guilbaud (1952) was the first to calculate the probability that there is no majority winner[24] for the case of three alternatives when the number of voters increases. He could show that the probability of a majority cycle goes up slightly with the number of voters and reaches a limiting value just under 9 per cent (0.0877). Should we then worry about the nonexistence of a majority winner? We probably should, because things look quite different when the number of alternatives increases (see, among others, Garman and Kamien 1968; Niemi and Weisberg 1968; Gehrlein and Fishburn 1976; Gehrlein 1983).

Several authors have attempted to give analytical representations for the probability of no majority winner (Gehrlein and Fishburn 1976, 1979; Gillett 1978; and others). Let n for the moment be the number of voters and m be the number of alternatives. Then we define $Q(m,n)$ to be the proportion of the $(m!)^n$ profiles for which there are no Condorcet winners. For the case of at least three alternatives, Kelly (1974b) has, among other things, proved that

---

[24] Note that only in the case of three alternatives, the existence of a majority winner is equivalent to the absence of a majority cycle. The concept of the existence of a majority (or Condorcet) winner is clearly different from the concept of the existence of a transitive majority preference relation. The likelihood for the existence of a majority winner will be larger than the likelihood of a transitive majority relation. To the best of our knowledge, Graaff (1965) was the first to look at the ratio of these two probabilities when the number of voters increases. More recently, Gehrlein (1990) has obtained representations for both probabilities in the case of four alternatives and n voters. Computed values for up to 19 voters are also given. For $n = 19$, for example, the probability for the existence of a majority winner is 0.844, the probability for the existence of a transitive majority relation is 0.7675. Gehrlein's results are based on the so-called 'impartial anonymous culture' condition, which means that all voter profiles are equally likely.

$$Q(m,n+1) < Q(m,n) \quad \text{for odd} \quad n \geq 3,$$
$$Q(m,n+1) > Q(m,n) \quad \text{for even} \quad n \geq 2.$$

Kelly (1986) has again drawn attention to the fact that the following relationships are still conjectures:

$$Q(m,n+2) > Q(m,n) \quad \text{for} \quad m \geq 3$$
$$\text{and} \quad n = 1 \quad \text{or} \quad n \geq 3,$$
$$Q(m+1,n) > Q(m,n) \quad \text{for} \quad m \geq 2$$
$$\text{and} \quad n = 3 \quad \text{or} \quad n \geq 5.$$

A rigorous proof of the first of these conjectures is now available for $m = 3$ and n either odd or sufficiently large and the second conjecture has also been proved for $m = 3$ (Fishburn, Gehrlein and Maskin 1979).[25] But the situation seems to become intractable when m increases. Therefore, approximations for $Q(m, n)$ when m and n are not relatively small have been developed. Table 3.1 shows an excerpt from a set of calculations given in Gehrlein (1983, 1998a).[26] The figures in table 3.1 indicate the probability of a majority winner; one minus the given probability is then the likelihood that there is no Condorcet winner. This probability, for example, is, as we have already mentioned, 0.0555 for $m = 3$ and $n = 3$ (see the entry in the first column and first row of table 3.1).

Table 3.1 clearly indicates that for m and n being odd, $Q(m, n)$ increases with increases in n. $Q(m,n)$ increases even faster when the number of alternatives grows. As

---

[25] For additional conjectures see Gehrlein's survey (1983, pp. 184–6).

[26] This is an excerpt from a table given in Gehrlein (1998a). Five decimal place entries are exact computations and three decimal place entries were computed with an approximation formula. The correct form of this formula can be found in Gehrlein's (1998a) paper, while the expression in Gehrlein (1983) contains several misprints. Under the impartial anonymous culture condition (see n. 24 above), Gehrlein (1998b) has derived a closed form representation for the probability that a Condorcet winner exists when $n = 3$. His calculations show that this probability quickly converges to the probability under the impartial culture condition as m increases. From $m = 10$ on, both probabilities are the same.

Table 3.1 Values for the probability of a majority winner

n/m	3	5	7	9	11	13	15	17
3	0.94444	0.84000	0.76120	0.70108	0.65356	0.61484	0.58249	0.55495
5	0.93056	0.80047	0.70424	0.63243	0.57682	0.53235	0.49583	0.46521
7	0.92498	0.78467	0.68168	0.60551	0.54703	0.50063	0.46280	0.43128
9	0.92202	0.77628	0.66976	0.59135	0.53144	0.48409	0.44564	0.413
11	0.92019	0.77108	0.66238	0.584	0.523	0.474	0.435	0.403
13	0.91893	0.76753	0.65736	0.578	0.516	0.467	0.428	0.395
15	0.91802	0.76496	0.65372	0.574	0.511	0.462	0.423	0.390
17	0.91733	0.76300	0.65095	0.571	0.508	0.458	0.419	0.386
19	0.91678	0.76146	0.64879	0.568	0.505	0.455	0.416	0.383
...								
Limit	0.91226	0.74869	0.63082	0.54547	0.48129	0.43131	0.39127	0.35844

became clear from Kelly's results mentioned above, the picture is somewhat different for an even number of voters. For $m = 3$ and $n = 4$, it is easy to show that $Q(m,n) = 0$. There *always* exists a Condorcet winner. For $m = 3$, the probability for the existence of a Condorcet winner is 0.99614 for $n = 6$, 0.99199 for $n = 8$ and 0.98822 for $n = 10$.[27] This, however, means that given m, the increase of the number of voters from odd to even always creates a 'local discontinuity' upwards in the general trend of the probability (for the existence of a Condorcet winner) to go down.

Is this general downwards trend the end of the story? It is not, so it seems, when we remember the fact that up to now we have only considered strict individual orderings. Furthermore, the impartial culture condition has been valid throughout the foregoing arguments. However, 'the equiprobability assumption *is* a very special one, and seems to involve a denial of society, in a significant sense' (Sen 1970, p. 164, emphasis in the original). Sen goes on to argue that there can be a fair amount of link-up between individual preferences. Williamson and Sargent (1967) have assumed in their approach that one of the logically possible preference orderings occurs with slightly greater frequency than any of the others.[28] Under these circumstances, the probability that the social relation will be transitive is much higher than under the equiprobability assumption. Or, alternatively, the probability of intransitivity goes down significantly (the authors have not examined the probability of the existence of a Condorcet winner). The probability of intransitivity decreases even more rapidly when the logically possible orderings are arranged according to their degree of similarity with some specified ordering, the likelihood of each ordering varying directly with its degree of similarity

---

[27] I am grateful to Claudia Lawrenz for doing these calculations.

[28] In the case of three alternatives and only strict orderings, one of the orderings, say $xPyPz$, would be assumed to occur with probability $1/6 + \varepsilon$ (where $0 < \varepsilon < 1/6$) and each of the remaining orderings would occur with probability $1/6 - \varepsilon/5$.

(or inversely with respect to its 'distance' from the specified ordering).

Fishburn and Gehrlein (1980) have relaxed the assumption that individuals are never indifferent between distinct alternatives. They show that the likelihood of the voting paradox decreases as individuals exhibit more indifference. This is not surprising. Remember, for example, that according to one of Inada's results the paradox vanishes completely when all individuals manifest dichotomous preferences. The result is important since individual indifference comes about quite naturally. Consequently, the figures in table 3.1 above may now appear in a somewhat different light. On the other hand, the likelihood of majority cycles increases (as was to be expected) when we admit instances of intransitivity in the individuals' preference relations.[29]

3.5 Simple games

The introduction of the concept of a simple game into the area of preference aggregation goes back to Guilbaud (1952) and Blau (1957). For a comprehensive study of simple games, the reader is referred to Shapley (1962). The analysis of simple games as collective choice rules is due to Bloomfield (1971, 1976), Bloomfield and Wilson (1972), Wilson (1972) and Peleg (1978, 1984).[30]

A coalition is a nonempty subset of N, the set of individuals. Let K be a coalition; xR_Ky means that for all $i \in K : xR_iy$, and xP_Ky means that for all $i \in K : xP_iy$. A coalition K is winning iff $\forall(R_1, \ldots, R_n), \forall x, y \in X : xP_Ky \rightarrow xPy$.

Definition. A simple game is an ordered pair $(N, \mathcal{W})$, where $\mathcal{W}$, the set of winning coalitions, satisfies:

---

[29] For the case of *individual* choices, Gehrlein (1994) has looked at the expected likelihood that an agent will have transitive preferences for pairwise choices on a set of three alternatives having n different attributes of comparison.

[30] See also Monjardet's (1969, 1978) contributions to this area.

$$K_1 \in W \quad \text{and} \quad K_1 \subset K_2 \rightarrow K_2 \in W.$$

This condition is called the monotonicity property for simple games. A simple game can be interpreted as a committee where N represents the set of members of the committee and W gives the set of coalitions that fully control the decisions of the committee.

Definition. Let (N, W) be a simple game. It is said to be proper if

$$K \in W \rightarrow N \backslash K \notin W.$$

It is said to be strong if

$$K \notin W \rightarrow N \backslash K \in W.$$

We now wish to relate the notion of a simple game to the concept of a collective choice rule.

Definition. A simple voting game is a triple (N, W, f) where (N, W) is a simple game and f, the collective choice rule, is a mapping from $\mathcal{A}^m$ to $\mathcal{A}$ such that $\forall(R_1, \ldots, R_n), \forall x, y \in X : xPy \leftrightarrow [\exists K \in W : xP_K y]$, where P is generated by f.

Note that we could also have defined a social preference relation R, $(\forall(R_1, \ldots, R_n), \forall x, y \in X : xRy \leftrightarrow [\exists K \in W : xR_K y])$. One can easily see that if (N, W) is a proper and strong simple game, the two definitions are equivalent.

A well-known example for a simple game is the voting system of the United Nations Security Council (see Riker and Ordeshook 1973). The Council consists of five permanent members and 10 nonpermanent members. In order to pass substantive motions nine votes are required, including the five permanent members. This game is proper since the complement of a winning coalition clearly is not winning. Is this game also strong? No, it is not because according to the rules neither the five permanent members, for example, nor the 10 nonpermanent members of the Council form a winning coalition. The strict majority rule which we defined at the beginning of section 3.2 above is a proper simple game. It is strong only if the total number of voters is odd.

3.5.1 Simple majority games

In this subsection we examine a slight modification[31] of the strict majority rule that was proposed by Dummett and Farquharson (1961).

Definition. A majority voting game is a simple voting game (N, W, f) where $W = \{K : [|K| > \frac{1}{2} \cdot |N|,$ when $|N|$ is odd] $\vee [(|K| > \frac{1}{2} \cdot |N|) \vee (|K| = \frac{1}{2} \cdot |N| \wedge 1 \in K)$ when $|N|$ is even]$\}$ and where f is a mapping from $\mathcal{B}'^n$ to $\mathcal{B}$. $|K|$ denotes the cardinality of K, $|N|$ is the number of voters, and voter 1 can be interpreted as the chairman having a tie-breaking vote as well as an ordinary vote.

One can easily see that this rule defines a strong and proper simple game. In the following, the sets $\mathcal{B}'$ in the definition shall be replaced by sets $\mathcal{E}'$ so that the domain of f will be $\mathcal{E}'^n$.

Definition. (a) Not-Strictly-Worst Value Restriction NSW (Dummett and Farquharson 1961). There exists an alternative in a given triple (x,y,z) such that it is not strictly worst in any preference ordering, i.e.
$\exists a, \exists b, \exists c$ such that for all $R_i : aR_ib \vee aR_ic$.
(b) Not-Strictly-Best Value Restriction NSB (Pattanaik 1970b).
There exists an alternative in a given triple (x,y,z) such that it is not strictly best in any ordering, i.e.
$\exists a, \exists b, \exists c$ such that for all $R_i : bR_ia \vee cR_ia$.
(c) Not-Strictly-Medium Value Restriction NSM (Pattanaik 1970 b).
There exists an alternative in a given triple (x,y,z) such that it is not strictly medium in any ordering, i.e.
$\exists a, \exists b, \exists c$ such that for no $i : [(bP_ia \wedge aP_ic) \vee (cP_ia \wedge aP_ib)]$.

We define the choice set $C(S)$ as the set $\{x \in S : xRy$ for all $y \in S\}$, where R is generated by rule f of the majority voting game.
We can now state the following theorems.

---

[31] This modification introduces a tie-breaking rule in the case of an even number of voters.

Theorem 12 (Dummett and Farquharson 1961). If the set of individual orderings $\mathcal{E}'$ satisfies condition *NSW* for every triple of alternatives belonging to a finite set S, the majority voting game (N,W,f) generates a nonempty choice set $C(S)$.

Theorem 13 (Pattanaik 1970b). If the set of individual orderings $\mathcal{E}'$ satisfies condition *NSB* for every triple of alternatives belonging to a finite set S, the majority voting game (N,W,f) generates a nonempty choice set $C(S)$.

The two theorems say that a nonempty choice set exists if all triples of alternatives satisfy the *NSW* restriction or if all triples satisfy the *NSB* restriction. A similar result is true for the *NSM* restriction only if the number of alternatives is not larger than three.

Theorem 14 (Pattanaik 1970b). If the individual orderings over a triple (x,y,z) satisfy condition NSM, then $C(\{x,y,z\})$ will be nonempty under the majority voting game (N,W,f).[32]

Two points should be made in relation to the results above. First, in contrast to theorem 4, for example, we cannot allow that the present restrictions vary from triple to triple. In other words, a nonempty choice set need not necessarily exist when some triples satisfy condition *NSW* and the other triples satisfy condition *NSB*. The following profile with four alternatives elucidates this point:

$$aI_1cP_1bI_1d,$$
$$bP_2aP_2dP_2c,$$
$$dP_3cP_3bP_3a.$$

In this example, the triple (a,b,c) satisfies *NSB* value restriction with respect to a; (a,b,d) satisfies *NSW* value restriction with respect to b; (a,c,d) satisfies *NSB* value restriction with respect to c; and (b,c,d) fulfils

---

[32] Pattanaik (1971, chap. 6) also proved theorems 12–14 for the method of nonminority decision (strict majority rule).

NSW value restriction with respect to *d*. However, the choice set over $\{a,b,c,d\}$ is empty.

Secondly, neither the *NSB* restriction nor the *NSW* value restriction is sufficient for collective transitivity. What is secured is that *f* is a social decision function.

3.5.2 Strong and proper simple games

As in the case of the majority games, only transitive individual preference relations are considered in this and the following subsection.

Definition. A strong and proper simple voting game is a simple voting game $(N,\mathcal{W},f)$ where $(N,\mathcal{W})$ is a strong and proper simple game and where *f* is a mapping from $\mathcal{B}^{\prime n}$ to $\mathcal{B}$.

As in subsection 3.5.1, we let the domain of *f* be $\mathcal{E}^{\prime n}$. Wilson (1972) analysed Arrow's general impossibility theorem within a game-theoretical framework. He could show that the winning coalitions in Arrow's theory meet the requirements for the winning coalitions in a strong and proper simple game. Using this structure, Wilson proved that either some individual constitutes a winning coalition,[33] or there exists a profile of individual preferences such that the corresponding social relations of strict and weak preference are cyclic and intransitive, which is Arrow's theorem. Wilson finally demonstrated that the condition of single-peakedness is sufficient for the existence of a transitive social preference relation generated by his collective choice rule. Salles (1975) expanded Wilson's analysis in so far as Sen's value restriction, a weaker exclusion condition than single-peakedness, and a new exclusion condition were taken into account. In the following, all individuals will be assumed to be concerned for every triple of alternatives.

---

[33] Note that within Wilson's axiomatic set-up, a subset of Arrow's conditions, a coalition is winning iff it intersects every winning coalition. Furthermore, Wilson proved the equivalence between winning and blocking coalitions.

Definition. Cyclical Indifferences CI (Salles 1975). For a triple (x, y, z), either there exist individuals whose preference orderings are $(xI_iy \land yP_iz) \lor (yI_iz \land zP_ix) \lor (zI_ix \land xP_iy)$, and these orderings are the only ones, or there exist individuals whose preference orderings are $(xP_iy \land yI_iz) \lor (yP_iz \land zI_ix) \lor (zP_ix \land xI_iy)$, and these orderings are the only ones.

Theorem 15 (Salles 1975). Iff the set of individual orderings $\mathcal{E}'$ satisfies for every triple of alternatives one of the exclusion conditions of value restriction and cyclical indifferences, every strong and proper simple voting game generates transitive social preferences (the collective choice rule f is a social welfare function).

We should note in passing that conditions ER and LA which are sufficient for the existence of a social ordering under the method of majority decision, are no longer sufficient under the present collective choice rules which clearly are more general than the majority rule.

3.5.3 Proper simple games

Definition. A proper simple voting game is a simple voting game $(N,\mathcal{W},f)$ where $(N,\mathcal{W})$ is a proper simple game and where f is defined on $\mathcal{B}^m$.

Again the analysis will be confined to choice rules f defined on $\mathcal{E}'^n$. In what follows we shall present a characterization of individual preference orderings such that every proper simple voting game generates a quasi-transitive social preference relation (the range of f is $\mathcal{D}$).

Definition. Cyclical Dependence CD (Salles 1976). If there exists an individual i whose preferences for a,b,c in (x,y,z) are $aP_ib \land bP_ic$, then
$$\neg[\exists j : (bP_jc \land cP_ja) \land \exists k : (cR_ka \land aR_kb)] \text{ and}$$
$$\neg[\exists j' : (bR_{j'}c \land cR_{j'}a) \land \exists k' : (cP_{k'}a \land aP_{k'}b)] \text{ and}$$
$$\neg[\exists j'' : (bP_{j''}c \land cI_{j''}a) \land \exists k'' : (cI_{k''}a \land aP_{k''}b)],$$
where individuals k and j' are concerned for (x,y,z).

This condition is such that certain types of Latin Squares are not allowed to occur.

Theorem 16 (Salles 1976). Iff the set of individual order-ings $\mathcal{E}'$ satisfies for every triple of alternatives one of the conditions of value restriction and cyclical dependence, every proper simple voting game is a social decision function of type QT (f has quasi-transitive values over every triple (x,y,z)).

Salles' proof of the theorem shows that the conditions of limited agreement, extremal restriction and antagonistic preferences are no longer sufficient for quasi-transitivity. This can be immediately seen for a three-person game with a winning coalition having at least two members and the following profile: xP_1yP_1z, yP_2zI_2x and zI_3xP_3y, yielding xPy, yPz and xIz. This example can also be used to show that, in the present case, it is not true that a violation of quasi-transitivity for some preference profile necessarily entails a violation of acyclicity under some number-distribution of individuals. The relation zPx cannot be gen-erated under the specified mechanism which is the strict majority rule. This is in contrast to an observation by Sen and Pattanaik (1969, p. 199) with respect to simple majority decision, where for a different preference profile, a violation of quasi-transitivity turns into a strict prefer-ence cycle for some number-distribution of voters. More precisely, let there be three individuals with the orderings xP_1yP_1z, yP_2zP_2x and zP_3xI_3y. The simple majority rule yields yPz, zPx and xIy which violates quasi-transitivity. If we now assume that two individuals each have the first and the third of the three orderings while the second ordering is still held by just one person, simple majority decision generates a strict preference cycle.

CHAPTER 4

ARROVIAN SOCIAL WELFARE FUNCTIONS, NONMANIPULABLE VOTING PROCEDURES AND STABLE GROUP DECISION FUNCTIONS

Arrow's impossibility theorem states that there exist no nondictatorial social welfare functions when the set of individual orderings is unrestricted. Gibbard (1973) and Satterthwaite (1973, 1975) proved that if all logically possible individual preference orderings are admissible, the only nonmanipulable voting procedures are dictatorial ones. There have been two lines of investigation to resolve the difficulties posed by these impossibility results. Path 1 proposed to choose a particular aggregation mechanism (such as the majority rule or some extension of this method) and then to look for domain conditions such that possibility results are obtained. This is what we were discussing throughout chapter 3 with respect to social welfare functions and related collective choice rules. Path 2 which was initiated by Maskin (1975, 1976) and, independently, by Kalai and Muller (1977), reversed the procedure. In these investigations, domains of individual orderings are characterized which admit n-person nondictatorial social welfare functions and n-person nondictatorial nonmanipulable voting procedures. To this line of research we now turn. We shall also return to the method of majority decision and see that among all aggregation schemes that fulfil a certain set of properties, simple majority voting is the only rule that is transitive on the widest class of domains.

4.1 Domains for Arrow-type social welfare functions and nonmanipulable voting schemes

We shall approach the current theme somewhat indirectly by first presenting and discussing the following two examples which can be found in Kalai, Muller and Satterthwaite (1979).

Example 1. Let $X = \{x_1, x_2, x_3, y_1, y_2, y_3\}$ and assume that there are at least three individuals. Consider the domain of preferences consisting of all n-tuples of orderings with the following characteristics: the sets $\{x_1, x_2, x_3\}$ and $\{y_1, y_2, y_3\}$ are free triples so that all logically possible orderings of the elements in these sets are permissible. Furthermore, all elements from $\{x_1, x_2, x_3\}$ are always arranged above all elements from $\{y_1, y_2, y_3\}$ in the admissible orderings, i.e. every individual ranks each x_i above each y_j for $i, j \in \{1, 2, 3\}$. It is well known that any Arrow-type social welfare function on this domain must have a dictator on each of the free triples. If we now construct a social aggregation procedure in the way that individual 1 is made dictator over $\{x_1, x_2, x_3\}$, individual 2 is made dictatorial over $\{y_1, y_2, y_3\}$, and unanimity determines the social rankings between x_i and $y_j, i, j \in \{1, 2, 3\}$, we have chosen a rule that satisfies Arrow's conditions I and P, and there is no dictator in Arrow's sense.

Example 2. Let X be as defined in example 1. This time the preference domain consists of all n-tuples of orderings such that the set $\{x_1, x_2, x_3\}$ is a free triple, every individual ranks each x_i in $\{x_1, x_2, x_3\}$ above each y_j in $\{y_1, y_2, y_3\}$ and the elements in the latter set are ranked unanimously in the descending order $y_1 P y_2 P y_3$. If we consider a social welfare function satisfying conditions I and P, there is a dictator on the free triple and via the Pareto condition, this person becomes dictatorial over the whole set X. So no Arrow social welfare function exists in this case.

In order to explain these two examples, we have to introduce some notation and definitions. We want to call a pair of distinct alternatives $x, y \in X$ trivial relative to the set of admissible preference orderings, if there is some individual i who has only one admissible preference over the pair $\{x, y\}$. Pairs which are not trivial are called nontrivial. Two nontrivial pairs $B = \{x, y\}$ and $C = \{c, z\}$ are said to be strongly connected if the cardinality

$|B \cup C| = 3$ and $B \cup C$ is a free triple. Thus B and C are strongly connected if they share an element in common and together form a free triple. Two pairs B and C are called connected if a finite sequence of pairs $B_1, B_2, \ldots, B_{n-1}, B_n$ with $B_1 = B$ and $B_n = C$ exists such that B_i and B_{i+1} are strongly connected for each $i = 1, 2, \ldots, n - 1$. We wish to say that there is a common preference domain if each person has the same set of admissible preferences. Finally, a set of admissible preference orderings is called saturating if (a) the set of alternatives contains at least two nontrivial pairs and (b) any two nontrivial pairs are connected.

The following theorem by Kalai, Muller and Satterthwaite establishes an illuminating result.

Theorem 17 (Kalai, Muller and Satterthwaite 1979). If a social welfare function f is defined on a common saturating preference domain and satisfies Arrow's independence condition and weak Pareto, then f is dictatorial.

The mechanism behind this result can be described as a local Arrovian approach (Bordes and Le Breton 1989). First in this procedure, free triples are identified; then a local version of Arrow's theorem is used to prove the existence of a dictator on a triple. One then shows a contagion property: that an individual's sphere of dictatorship expands by a connection process to other free triples, and finally to the whole set of alternatives. Coming back to the two examples above, in the first case, the domain of preferences is not saturating. The two triples are free, but pairs from each triple are not connected. Therefore, the theorem above is not applicable and, as pointed out, a nondictatorial Arrow social welfare function can be established. In the second case, the domain is saturating. The set $\{x_1, x_2, x_3\}$ is a free triple, all pairs involving $\{y_1, y_2, y_3\}$ are trivial and all preference relations between the two sets are trivial as well. Therefore, in the second example, the theorem above applies.

Kalai, Muller and Satterthwaite show furthermore that if the space of alternatives is $R_+^n, n \geq 1$, where each dimension represents a different public good, and if each individual's preference ordering is restricted to be convex, continuous and strictly monotonic (the standard assumptions in micro-economic theory), Arrow's impossibility result for social welfare functions holds. Le Breton and Weymark (1996) provide various other examples for Arrow-type impossibilities. The assumption in the theorem above that the preference domain is common and saturating is merely sufficient, and not necessary in order to generate a dictatorial welfare function. Le Breton and Weymark present an example where the preference domain is common but not saturating; yet there is dictatorship. They also give an example which shows that the common preference domain assumption is essential for the result in theorem 17: there exist saturating preference domains such that a non-dictatorial social welfare function exists.

Let there be two individuals and let the set of alternatives be $X = \{x_1, x_2, x_3, x_4\}$. Furthermore, allow both persons to have unrestricted preferences on $\{x_1, x_2, x_3\}$ and let any pair of alternatives in this subset be nontrivial. However, pairs formed with x_4 as one of the alternatives are trivial and it is assumed that on the trivial pairs, the two individuals have opposite strict preferences: $x_4 P_1 x_i$ for $i \in \{1,2,3\}$ and $x_i P_2 x_4$ for $i \in \{1,2,3\}$. Le Breton and Weymark design a social welfare function that sets xRy iff xR_1y when $x, y \in \{x_1, x_2, x_3\}$ and xPx_4 when $x \in \{x_1, x_2, x_3\}$. So person 1 is made a dictator on $\{x_1, x_2, x_3\}$ and person 2 dictates on all the trivial pairs. For obvious reasons, person 1's dictatorship does not spread to the set X. This social welfare function satisfies independence, weak Pareto, and nondictatorship on a preference domain that is saturating but not common.

The next step is much more ambitious. Are there necessary and sufficient conditions on the domain of preferences such that an Arrovian social welfare function exists? Maskin (1975, 1976) and Kalai and Muller (1977) proved a remarkable result which greatly simplifies the analysis: There exists an n-person social welfare function (voting procedure) for a given domain iff there exists a 2-person social welfare function (voting procedure) for the same domain. Thus the question of domain restriction can be dealt with independently of the number of individuals in the society.

In the subsequent model, only strict orderings will be considered. Let X denote a set of mutually exclusive social alternatives with at least two elements and let Σ denote the set of all strict preference orderings on X. The elements of X are to be viewed as allocations of public goods. Furthermore, let $\Omega \subset \Sigma$ denote a nonempty subset of Σ. The elements of Ω represent the admissible preference orderings in society N. For any $n \geq 2$, Ω^n stands for the set of all n-tuples of preference orderings from Ω, with $(P_1, \ldots, P_n)$ being a typical element of Ω^n.

Definition. An n-person social welfare function on Ω is a mapping $f : \Omega^n \to \Sigma$ which satisfies the following two conditions. (1) The Weak Pareto Condition (Unanimity). For all $(P_1, \ldots, P_n) \in \Omega^n$, for all $x, y \in X$ and all $i \in N$: $xP_iy \to xf(P_1, \ldots, P_n)y$. (2) Independence of Irrelevant Alternatives. For all $x, y \in X$, all $(P_1, \ldots, P_n)$, $(P'_1, \ldots, P'_n) \in \Omega^n : [xP_iy \leftrightarrow xP'_iy$ for all $i \in N] \to [xf(P_1, \ldots, P_n)y \leftrightarrow xf(P'_1, \ldots, P'_n)y]$.

The function f is called dictatorial if there exists an $i \in N$ such that for every pair $x, y \in X$ and for all $(P_1, \ldots, P_n) \in \Omega^n, f (P_1, \ldots, P_n) = P_i$. Maskin as well as Kalai and Muller used this notion of dictatorship which is known from Arrow's analysis. Note that an aggregation mechanism where one individual is socially decisive over the pairs in one set of alternatives, a second individual is decisive over all the other pairs of social states while all other persons are decisive over no pair at all, is not dictatorial in the sense just defined and thus satisfies Arrow's nondictatorship condition stated in chapter 2. This type of aggregation procedure which the reader may not find particularly appealing (see again example 1 at the beginning of this chapter) should be kept in mind when Kalai and Muller's domain assumption is defined next.

Let $T = \{(x,y) \in X^2 : x \neq y\}$, $TR = \{(x,y) \in T :$ there exist no $P_1, P_2 \in \Omega$ such that xP_1y and $yP_2x\}$ and $NTR = T - TR$. Thus T consists of all distinct ordered pairs, TR represents the set of trivial pairs (either xPy for all $P \in \Omega$ or yPx for all $P \in \Omega$) and NTR consists of the nontrivial ordered pairs (there exist $P_1, P_2 \in \Omega$ such that xP_1y and yP_2x).[1] With these definitions Kalai and Muller's decomposability condition can be defined.

Definition. Nondictatorial Decomposability (Kalai and Muller 1977).[2] The set of preferences $\Omega \subset \Sigma$ is nondictatorially decomposable (ND) with respect to a domain Ω^n if there exist two sets S_1 and S_2 with $TR \subsetneqq S_i \subsetneqq T$, $i \in \{1, 2\}$, having the following properties:

(a) For all $(x, y) \in NTR, (x,y) \in S_1$ iff $(y,x) \notin S_2$.
(b) For all nontrivial pairs the following is true for $i = 1, 2$:
   (b1) If there are $P_1, P_2 \in \Omega$ with xP_1yP_1z and yP_2zP_2x, then $(x, y) \in S_i$ implies $(x, z) \in S_i$;
   (b2) If there are $P_1, P_2 \in \Omega$ with xP_1yP_1z and yP_2zP_2x, then $(z,x) \in S_i$ implies $(y,x) \in S_i$;
   (b3) If there is a $P \in \Omega$ with $xPyPz$, then $(x,y) \in S_i$ and $(y,z) \in S_i$ imply $(x,z) \in S_i$.

S_i is the set of pairs for which individual i is decisive. Nondictatorial decomposability states that there are two persons with some power of decisiveness and clause (a) makes sure that there is no clash of decisiveness over pairs between the two persons.

Theorem 18 (Kalai and Muller 1977). There exists a non-dictatorial n-person social welfare function on Ω iff Ω satisfies condition ND.

It may be of interest to note that Kalai and Muller's domain condition is a restriction on permissible preferences for individuals. The conditions discussed in chapter 3 were restrictions on combinations of individual orderings (profile restrictions). It can, however, be shown that a set of single-peaked preferences (which has to be defined relative to some particular linear ordering) satisfies property ND

---

[1] Note that the present use of the attributes 'trivial' and 'nontrivial' is different from the one introduced earlier in this chapter.
[2] This definition is slightly different from the one given by the authors. See, however, their remark on p. 465 of the paper and Blair and Muller (1983, p. 48).

and therefore admits nondictatorial n-person social welfare functions (Kalai and Muller 1977, p. 466).

There are analogues both to the Kalai–Muller–Satterthwaite theorem and to the Kalai–Muller result for the case that the social alternatives are allocations of private goods only and not, as discussed above, allocations of purely public goods. Let us begin with an analogue to the former theorem. For situations that involve private dimensions alone, we shall assume that the set of alternatives X is Cartesian, i.e. $X = \prod_{i=1}^{n} X_i$, where X_i describes that part of the social alternative relevant for i (i's consumption set, let's say). We shall further assume that individuals are selfish which means that they care only about their own component in a social alternative. We shall write D_i for individual i's selfish preference domain on the Cartesian set X, where $D_i \subset \mathcal{E}$ for all $i \in N$, and $D = \prod_{i=1}^{n} D_i$ is the Cartesian preference domain. For the following result by Bordes and Le Breton (1989), it is not necessary to assume a common preference domain, i.e. it is not necessary to have $D_i = D_j$ for all $i, j \in N$.

Above, we have already defined what it means for a set of admissible preference orderings to be saturating. However, for the Bordes–Le Breton theorem, a refinement of this property is necessary. This is mainly owing to a specific treatment of nonindifferent trivial pairs in the case of selfish preferences. We need two more definitions.

Definition. Individual i's selfish preference domain D_i is supersaturating iff: (1) D_i is saturating; (2) for all nontrivial pairs x, y with respect to D_i in X, there exist $u, v \in X$ such that $u, v \notin \{x, y\}$, and $\{x,y,u\}$, $\{x,y,v\}$, $\{x,u,v\}$, and $\{y,u,v\}$ are free triples with respect to D_i. A preference domain D is supersaturating if D_i is supersaturating for all $i \in N$.

Bordes and Le Breton show that if D is supersaturating, any two nontrivial pairs are connected. Border (1983) has demonstrated that when the set of alternatives is Cartesian and the domain of preferences is selfish and supersaturating, an Arrovian social welfare function exists.

Since Border's construction of a social welfare function helps to clarify the next result, we shall present the following details.

Example 3. Suppose X is both a Cartesian set of alternatives and a connected subset of a Euclidean space. For each person i (there are only two individuals), there is a selfish preference ordering that is strictly monotonic in own consumption, i.e. each individual's preference domain is selfish. It can be shown that each D_i and thus the overall preference domain D is supersaturating (Le Breton and Weymark 1996, p. 49). Now consider the following partition of X: $A_1 = \{x \in X | x^1 \neq 0 \text{ and } x^2 \neq 0\}, A_2 = \{x \in X | x^1 \neq 0 \text{ and } x^2 = 0\}, A_3 = \{x \in X | x^1 = 0 \text{ and } x^2 \neq 0\}$, and $A_4 = \{0\}$. In A_1, both persons consume a positive amount of at least one good. In each of the other sets, at least one person gets nothing. Border's suggested social welfare function is defined as follows:

$$xRy \text{ iff } xR_2y \text{ for } x,y \in A_1 \text{ and for } x,y \in A_3,$$
$$xRy \text{ iff } xR_1y \text{ for } x,y \in A_2, \text{ and}$$
$$xPy \text{ iff } x \in A_i \text{ and } y \in A_j \text{ with } i < j.$$

This social welfare function can be seen to be non-dictatorial. Person 2 is dictating on alternatives in A_1. However, this person is not an Arrovian dictator, since if $x \in A_3$ and $y \in A_2$, we have xP_2y, yet according to the above specification, the social preference is yPx. It can also be verified that this social welfare function satisfies weak Pareto and the independence condition.

Let us now introduce the second definition, the notion of a hypersaturating preference domain.

Definition. Individual i's preference domain is hypersaturating iff: (1) D_i is supersaturating and (2) for all pairs $\{x,y\}$ in X that are trivial for i and such that xP_iy for all orderings $R_i \in D_i$, there exist $u \in X$ and $R'_i \in D_i$ such that $xP'_iuP'_iy$, where the pairs $\{x, u\}$ and $\{y, u\}$ are nontrivial for i. A preference domain D is hypersaturating if D_i is hypersaturating for all $i \in N$.

Clause (2) in the last definition formulates a separation condition for trivial pairs. A trivial pair $\{x,y\}$ is separable for person i if i is not indifferent between x and y and there exists an admissible ordering for i and an alternative u such that u is on an indifference curve lying between the indifference curves through x and y and such that $\{x,u\}$ and $\{y,u\}$ are nontrivial pairs for i.

Theorem 19 (Bordes and Le Breton 1989). Suppose X is a Cartesian set of alternatives. If a social welfare function f is defined on a preference domain D that is both selfish and hypersaturating and if f satisfies Arrow's independence condition and weak Pareto, then f is dictatorial.

If for each $i \in N$, D_i is the set of all selfish, continuous, strictly monotonic (in own consumption), and convex preference orderings and if each consumption set X_i is some strictly positive orthant, then this preference domain is hypersaturating. However, the classical domain of microeconomic preferences for private goods admits the existence of an Arrow social welfare function if the origin is included in the individual consumption sets. As seen from example 3, the latter result has to do with the fact that, with the origin being included in the consumption set, it may not be possible to separate some nonindifferent trivial pairs. In figure 4.1, which depicts a two-dimensional case, the trivial pair $\{x,y\}$ is separable for the person

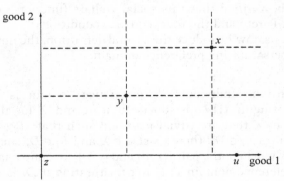

Figure 4.1

54

considered. However, for that person, it is not possible to separate the nonindifferent trivial pair $\{z,u\}$. Note, however, that according to the theorem above, dictatorship still holds on the subset of alternatives obtained by deleting the origin from each individual's X_i.[3]

---

[3] In recent years, there has been an avalanche of papers along the lines of the Kalai–Muller–Satterthwaite and the Bordes–Le Breton analyses, mostly generating impossibility results. Bordes and Le Breton (1990) have shown for the case where each social alternative is composed of private components and a public component ('the mixed case') that Arrow's inconsistency persists (see also Redekop 1996 for mixed goods in dynamic economic environments). Bordes and Le Breton assume that individuals look only at their own component and the public component. They call their domain restriction 'ultrasaturating', actually a combination of elements from the saturating and hypersaturating domains, adapted to the mixed case. Bordes and Le Breton argue that standard economic domains with infinitely divisible private and public goods and such that individual preferences satisfy continuity, convexity and monotonicity are ultrasaturating. Note that in the authors' set-up, the private goods vectors exclude the origin.

In their paper, an example is given for what Kelly (1994) has called 'the Bordes–Le Breton exceptional case'. Clearly, there exists no Arrow social welfare function on a preference domain which is the n-fold Cartesian product of the set of all possible linear orderings on a set X. The same holds true when one goes from linear orderings to weak orderings on set X. However, the authors have constructed an intermediate domain where the relation of total indifference among all alternatives is added to the set of linear orderings. If this relation of complete indifference occurs in a profile of the intermediate domain, i.e. at least one individual chooses to be completely indifferent among all options, the dictatorship switches from person 1 (who dictates over profiles with only linear orderings) to person 2.

Redekop (1991) considered the possibility of making further restrictions on the individual preference domains, beyond the restrictions of monotonicity and continuity. His main findings were that in order to guarantee the existence of Arrow social welfare functions, the set of admissible individual preferences must be topologically small (the domain must be nowhere dense in the Kannai topology). An analogous result was obtained by Redekop (1993) in the case of convex or homothetic preferences. Further (mostly negative) results have been obtained by Border (1983), Bordes and Le Breton (1989) and Campbell (1990, 1992), among others. Le Breton (1997) discusses various possibility results for the case that both the domain of preferences and the domain of feasible sets are restricted. An extensive survey of this Arrovian literature is to be found in Le Breton and Weymark (2000).

Domain conditions in social choice theory

Kalai and Ritz (1980) have proved an analogue to the Kalai–Muller theorem above for the case that every social alternative is composed of a bundle of private alternatives only and each individual i is concerned with the ith component of each social alternative alone. Kalai and Ritz assumed that all the individual sets of private alternatives and all the domains of admissible orderings are the same. The authors proved the independence between the group size and the existence of an Arrow-type social welfare function and they characterized all the restricted domains which admit such functions.

Kalai and Ritz were criticized both for assuming a common preference domain and for requiring the set of private alternatives to be the same for all members of society. The main criticism, however, pointed to the fact that only strong orderings are admissible in their model. If the possibility of indifference is allowed, their results no longer hold.[4]

Ritz (1983) was able to generalize the Kalai–Ritz approach in so far as individuals may indeed be indifferent among their private alternatives, and each person may have a different set of permissible preferences. Ritz proved first that a set of n restricted domains of preferences admits an Arrow-type social welfare function independently of the number of individuals and then characterized all the sets of restricted domains admitting Arrow-type social welfare functions. We shall briefly sketch his second result.

For every $i \in N$, let A_i be the set of private alternatives available to person i (A_i is assumed to be a set of discrete elements with $|A_i| \geq 2$). We let $A^{(n)} = A_1 \times A_2 \times \ldots \times A_n$. Let $D_i \subset \mathcal{E}$ denote individual i's restricted domain of admissible selfish preferences and let $D = \prod_{i=1}^{n} D_i$ be the

---

[4] Bordes and Le Breton (1989) write that in most economic domains, indifference is systematically implied by continuity of preferences which means that the Kalai–Ritz results cannot be applied to classical problems in welfare economics (pp. 264–5). Actually, the authors were well aware of these deficiencies (Kalai and Ritz 1980, p. 25). A limited amount of individual indifference is indeed permitted in one of the aggregation procedures characterized by Blair and Muller (1983).

preference domain of the social welfare function. In the light of his first result, Ritz can confine himself to characterizing all the sets of two restricted domains of preferences admitting two-person Arrow-type social welfare functions.

Let $F = \{(X,Y) \in A^{(2)} \times A^{(2)}|$ for some $R_1 \in D_1, x_1 P_1 y_1\}$. F contains all the ordered pairs of alternatives that are feasible and where individual 1 strictly prefers X to Y owing to his own components. Ritz refers to F as the feasible set. Let $C = \{(X,Y) \in F|$ there exists an $R_2 \in D_2$ such that $y_2 P_2 x_2\}$. C contains all the ordered pairs from F over which individual 2 can create a conflict of interest with individual 1, since person 2 prefers Y to X. C is called the conflict set. Now $K \subseteq A^{(2)} \times A^{(2)}$ is said to be closed under decisiveness implications if the following conditions hold for every $X,Y,Z \in A^{(2)}$:

(1a) If for some $R_1 \in D_1, x_1 P_1 y_1 R_1 z_1$ and $(X,Y) \in K$, then $(X,(z_1,y_2)) \in K$.

(1b) If for some $R_1 \in D_1, x_1 R_1 y_1 P_1 z_1$ and $(Y,Z) \in K$, then $((x_1,y_2),Z) \in K$.

(1c) If for some $R_1 \in D_1, x_1 P_1 y_1 P_1 z_1$ and $(X,Y),(Y,Z) \in K$, then $(X,Z) \in K$.

(2a) If for some $R_2 \in D_2, x_2 P_2 y_2 R_2 z_2$ and $(Z,X) \in K$, then $((z_1,y_2),X) \in K$.

(2b) If for some $R_2 \in D_2, x_2 R_2 y_2 P_2 z_2$ and $(Z,X) \in K$, then $(Z,(x_1,y_2)) \in K$.

(2c) If for some $R_2 \in D_2, x_2 P_2 y_2 P_2 z_2$ and $(Z,X) \in K$, then either $(Z,Y) \in K$ or $(Y,X) \in K$ (or both).

$D^{(2)} = D_1 \times D_2$ is said to be decomposable if there is a K which is closed under decisiveness implications. $D^{(2)}$ is said to have a nontrivial decomposition if it is decomposable with a K such that $(F - C) \subsetneqq K \subsetneqq F$. Intuitively, K contains, once a social welfare function exists, all the ordered pairs of social alternatives over which the first individual is decisive. Thus $K \subsetneqq F$ guarantees that this person is not a dictator, while $(F - C) \subsetneqq K$ guarantees that the second individual is not a dictator either.

Theorem 20 (Ritz 1983). $D^{(2)}$ admits a two-person Arrow social welfare function iff it has a nontrivial decomposition.

Ritz (1985) generalized this last result further when he considered situations where each social state is a combination of private and public alternatives. Some parts of each social alternative are assigned separately to individuals while other parts affect all the individuals together. Again, individuals may be indifferent among alternatives and individuals need not be symmetric in their private alternatives sets and in the sets of admissible orderings. Ritz characterized the sets of restricted domains of individual preferences that admit two-person Arrow social welfare functions. In the earlier results by Kalai and Muller, by Kalai and Ritz, and by Ritz it was always the case that if a restricted domain of preferences admitted a k-person Arrow social welfare function for a finite k greater than one, then it admitted an n-person Arrow social welfare function for any given finite n. A similar result for the case of private and public alternatives has not been achieved.

The close logical relationship between the existence of an Arrow social welfare function and the existence of a nonmanipulable voting procedure was analysed by Gibbard and Satterthwaite in the papers already mentioned, but also, among others, by Maskin (1975), Blin and Satterthwaite (1978) and Schmeidler and Sonnenschein (1978). Let us assume that it is known *a priori* that the preference orderings of all individuals in a given society satisfy the same characteristic (or peculiarity), in other words, the true preferences as well as the stated preferences of all individuals manifest a particular property. The question then arises whether domain conditions on individual orderings can be formulated such that an n-person nondictatorial and nonmanipulable voting procedure exists. Set X is supposed to be finite in the sequel.

Definition. An n-person voting procedure is a function $F : \Omega^n \times \Gamma \to X$, where Γ is the set of all nonempty subsets of X. We want F to fulfil the following properties. (i) Feasibility. For every $\gamma \in \Gamma$ and every $(P_1, \ldots, P_n) \in \Omega^n, F((P_1, \ldots, P_n), \gamma) \in \gamma$. (ii) Consistency. For every $(P_1, \ldots, P_n) \in \Omega^n$ and every $\gamma \in \Gamma$, if $\gamma' \subset \gamma$ and $F((P_1, \ldots, P_n), \gamma) \in \gamma'$, then $F((P_1, \ldots, P_n), \gamma') = F((P_1, \ldots, P_n), \gamma)$. (iii) Pareto Condition. For every $(P_1, \ldots, P_n) \in \Omega^n$ and every $\gamma \in \Gamma$, if $x, y \in \gamma$ and $x P_i y$ for all $i \in N$, then $y \neq F((P_1, \ldots, P_n), \gamma)$.

F is called dictatorial if there exists an individual $i \in N$ such that for every $(P_1, \ldots, P_n) \in \Omega^n$ and every $\gamma \in \Gamma, F((P_1, \ldots, P_n), \gamma) P_i y$ for every $y \in \gamma$ with $y \neq F((P_1, \ldots, P_n), \gamma)$.

F is manipulable if there exists a $\gamma \in \Gamma$ and $(P_1, \ldots, P_n)$, $(P'_1, \ldots, P'_n) \in \Omega^n$ such that for some $i \in N, P_i \neq P'_i$, for all $j \neq i, P_j = P'_j$ and $F((P'_1, \ldots, P'_n), \gamma) P_i F((P_1, \ldots, P_n), \gamma)$.

Kalai and Muller could show that the domain restriction which guarantees the existence of a nondictatorial n-person social welfare function secures the existence of a nonmanipulable voting procedure (so that the close logical relationship between the existence of both aggregation schemes becomes again visible).

Theorem 21 (Kalai and Muller 1977). There exists on Ω an n-person nondictatorial nonmanipulable voting procedure which satisfies properties (i), (ii) and (iii) iff Ω fulfils the condition of nondictatorial decomposability (ND).

Again, a set of single-peaked preferences guarantees existence, in this case the existence of an n-person nondictatorial nonmanipulable voting mechanism (see also Moulin 1980, 1988 chap. 10 and section 4.3 below). It should be mentioned in passing that Ritz (1983, 1985) has proved theorems similar to the result in theorem 21 for the case of private alternatives and the case of mixed alternatives.

As we have seen, Kalai and Muller's aggregation procedures are nondictatorial. However, for societies with more than two individuals, these decision rules are hardly acceptable. Two individuals are socially decisive over all pairs of alternatives, the rest of the society has no decisive power at all. Therefore, Blair and Muller (1983) proposed a class of decision schemes for which the distribution of power is somewhat more egalitarian: It is required that no voter be 'inessential' in the sense that he (or she) is completely deprived of power. Strengthening the property of nondictatorship to the requirement that all members of society are essential has a nontrivial effect on the set of domains for which Arrow-type social welfare functions or nonmanipulable voting procedures exist. In their analysis, Blair and Muller assume that different individuals may have different sets of admissible orderings. Therefore, if Ω_i denotes the admissible set of strict orderings of individual i, where, for all i, $\Omega_i \subset \Sigma$, $\prod_i \Omega_i$ is the set of n-tuples of admissible orderings for the society, with $(P_1, \ldots, P_n)$ being a typical element of $\Pi\Omega_i$. An Arrow social welfare function is canonically defined as a mapping $f : \Pi\Omega_i \rightarrow \Sigma$ that satisfies the weak Pareto condition and the condition of independence of irrelevant alternatives.

Definition. A social welfare function is said to be essential iff for all i, there exist a profile $(P_1, \ldots, P_n) \in \Pi\Omega_i$, an ordering $P_i' \in \Omega_i$ and a pair $x,y \in X$ such that $xf(P_1, \ldots, P_n)y$ and $yf(P_1, \ldots, P_{i-1}, P_i', P_{i+1}, \ldots, P_n)x$. A voting procedure is essential iff for all i, there exist a profile $(P_1, \ldots, P_n) \in \Pi\Omega_i$, an ordering $P_i' \in \Omega_i$ and a set $\gamma \in \Gamma$ such that $F((P_1, \ldots, P_n), \gamma) \neq F((P_1, \ldots, P_{i-1}, P_i', P_{i+1}, \ldots, P_n), \gamma)$.

We see that individual i is essential under some aggregation mechanism iff for a set of admissible voters' preferences, an admissible change in that person's preferences would alter the social outcome in the case of a voting procedure and would reverse the strict social preference in the case of a social welfare function (note that social indifference is excluded by assumption). Obviously, essentiality is a stronger condition than nondictatorship.

Let G, G' be coalitions of individuals among the members of society N. A social welfare function is monotonic iff for all x,y and for all coalitions G, if xP_iy for all $i \in G$ implies $xf(P_1, \ldots, P_n)y$ then $xP_i'y$ for all $i \in G' \supset G$ implies $xf(P_1', \ldots, P_n')y$.

We can now define the property of essential decomposability which will guarantee the existence of essential aggregation rules.

Definition. Essential Decomposability (Blair and Muller 1983). The set of ordered pairs of distinct alternatives is essentially decomposable (*ED*) with respect to a domain $\Pi\Omega_i$ iff for all such pairs $x,y \in X$, there exists a nonempty set $W(x, y)$ of coalitions $G \subset N$ such that

(1) For all coalitions G, if xP_iy for all $i \in G$ with $P_i \in \Omega_i$ and yP_jx for all $j \in N \backslash G$ with $P_j \in \Omega_j$, then $G \in W(x,y)$ iff $N \backslash G \notin W(y,x)$.

(2) For all coalitions G and G' such that $G \subset G', G \in W(x,y)$ implies $G' \in W(x,y)$.

(3) For all $i \in N$, there exist a pair x,y and a coalition G such that if xP_iy and yP_ix are admissible preferences of $i, G \in W(x,y)$ and $G \backslash \{i\} \notin W(x,y)$.

(4) For all x,y,z, if $G \in W(x,y), G' \in W(y,z), U \equiv \{i \in G : zPxPy$ is not admissible for $i\}, V \equiv \{i \in G' : yPzPx$ is not admissible for $i\}, xP_iy$ for all $i \in G$ and $P_i \in \Omega_i, yP_iz$ for all $i \in G'$ and $P_i \in \Omega_i$, and zP_ix for all $i \in N \backslash G \backslash G'$ and $P_i \in \Omega_i$, then $\emptyset \neq U \cup V \cup (G \cap G') \in W(x,z)$.

With $W(x,y)$ being the set of all coalitions that are winning over the ordered pair (x,y), clauses (1) and (2) in this definition should be evident from what we said about simple games in section 3.5. Clause (3) requires that each individual i be pivotal (and therefore essential) in some minimal winning coalition for some pair of alternatives. Clause (4) essentially formulates a domain restriction. It requires that if there are winning coalitions for the ordered pairs (x,y) and (y,z), there also be a nonempty winning coalition for the pair (x,z).

Theorem 22 (Blair and Muller 1983). There exists an n-person essential monotonic Arrow social welfare function iff the set of ordered pairs is essentially decomposable with respect to the domain $\Pi\Omega_i$.

For the case of two persons and under the assumption that the sets of admissible orderings are all identical, Blair and Muller have proved the equivalence of the Kalai–Muller decomposability condition and essential decomposability as well as the equivalence of nondictatorship and two-person essentiality. This equivalence no longer holds when individuals have different sets of admissible preferences. Let Ω_1 only contain the strict ordering xP_1yP_1z, Ω_2 only contain zP_2yP_2x and let the social outcome via $f(P_1,P_2)$ be $yPzPx$. There obviously is no dictatorship, but neither individual can affect the social ordering.

Theorem 23 (Blair and Muller 1983).[5] There exists an n-person essential individually nonmanipulable voting procedure iff the set of ordered pairs satisfies condition ED with respect to the domain $\Pi\Omega_i$.

One should notice that Maskin's and Kalai and Muller's nice result on the irrelevance of the number of voters does not hold for the present class of essential social welfare functions.

One final word on the analysis above. Blair and Muller raised the question whether their own result as well as those by Kalai and Muller, by Kalai and Ritz, and by Ritz are possibility theorems or basically impossibility results. In other words: How large are nondictatorial domains? We wish to look at this question for the case in which all individuals have the same set of admissible preference orderings ($\Omega_i = \Omega$ for all i).

Let us assume that there are k alternatives. Set Ω is said to contain an inseparable ordered pair if there is some nontrivial ordered pair (x,y) such that for no $P \in \Omega$ and no $z \in X$, $xPzPy$ (see also Muller and Satterthwaite 1985). Kim and Roush (1980, 1981) have shown that for the class of domains with an inseparable ordered pair, Ω cannot contain more than $\frac{k!}{2} + (k-1)!$ orderings. Any Ω^n such that Ω contains an inseparable ordered pair satisfies the property of nondictatorial decomposability. Therefore, if Ω contains

---

[5] The authors have a third result on group–nonmanipulable voting procedures. Note that the notions of individual manipulability and group manipulability of a voting procedure are completely equivalent in the context of essentiality.

an inseparable ordered pair, a nondictatorial n-person social welfare function exists. For the set of single-peaked preferences, for example, there exists an inseparable ordered pair.

The nondictatorial social welfare function which Kalai and Ritz (1978) proposed makes individual 1 a dictator on all pairs of alternatives except (x,y), for which the majority rule could be decisive, or any dictator different from person 1. Blair and Muller suggest a particular decision rule for (x,y): $xf(P_1,\ldots,P_n)y$ iff xP_iy for all $i \in N$. This decision scheme is not only nondictatorial, it is essential as well (at least with respect to the pair (x,y)). Let person 1 prefer x to y, then every other individual has veto power over (x,y). Thus x is socially chosen iff xP_jy for all $j \in \{2,\ldots,n\}$. If, however, some $\ell \in \{2,\ldots,n\}$ prefers y to x, y is socially picked. Consequently, the Kalai–Ritz property of the existence of an inseparable ordered pair, combined with this decision scheme, implies essential decomposability, and according to the result of Kim and Roush (1980, 1981), $\frac{k!}{2} + (k-1)!$ is the size of the largest Ω compatible with property ED. Blair and Muller remark that with $k!$ logically possible orderings over k alternatives, there exist essential domains with more than half of all possible orderings being admissible, 'a striking positive result' in their words.

4.2 Robustness of the majority rule

In n. 2 of chapter 3, we referred to May's (1952) axiomatization of the method of simple majority decision. May provided a complete characterization of the majority rule, using the conditions of anonymity (the social outcome does not depend on which individual expresses which preference), neutrality (if alternatives x and y, and z and w, respectively, are preferencewise arranged in an identical way in two profiles, the social relation between x and y in the first profile should be exactly the same as the relation between z and w in the second profile) and positive responsiveness (a change in favour of x in only one individual's preference with respect to alternatives x and y is sufficient for a change from social indifference to social preference between x and y). Note that neutrality, as used here, is stronger than Arrow's independence condition, and neutrality and positive responsiveness together imply the Pareto rule. Therefore, the simple majority rule fulfils three of Arrow's four axioms. Unrestricted domain as the fourth requirement may, as we have seen, yield an intransitive social preference.

Maskin (1995) and Dasgupta and Maskin (1998) have come up with a characterization of simple majority voting that is different in perspective from May's seminal work.[6] The two authors focus on the widest domains of preferences on which the majority rule is defined and they offer a defence of this voting rule in terms of a criterion they call 'robustness'.

For which restricted domains of individual preferences does a voting scheme such as the majority rule become an Arrow social welfare function? For the case of individual weak orderings, we have seen in chapter 3 that there is not a unique answer. The situation becomes simpler when we require that all individual orderings be strict and that, in addition, there be an odd number of voters. Then we know that Sen's (1966) value restriction condition is necessary and sufficient for the method of majority decision to be an Arrow social welfare function. Maskin (1995) has now shown the following.

Let f be any collective choice rule that is anonymous, neutral and positively responsive (and therefore fulfils the Pareto condition). Given the two requirements of oddness and strict individual preferences, if f is transitive on a particular domain, then the simple majority rule is transitive on this domain as well. Moreover, unless f itself is the simple majority rule, there exists a domain of individual orderings on which majority rule is transitive but f is not. Among all aggregation rules that fulfil the properties dis-

---

[6] Campbell and Kelly (2000) present yet another characterization of simple majority voting for an arbitrary, but finite number of voters. Their proofs look at the family of coalitions that are almost decisive for the social choice function. Campbell and Kelly do without the neutrality condition and work with a weaker transitivity requirement.

cussed above, the simple majority rule is the only one that is transitive on the widest class of domains. In this sense, the majority rule is robust.

More precisely, let there be an odd number of voters. Again, let Σ denote the set of all strict orderings on X, with $\Omega \subset \Sigma$ denoting a nonempty subset of Σ.

Theorem 24 (Maskin 1995). Let f be an n-person collective choice rule that satisfies anonymity, neutrality and the Pareto condition. Suppose that f is transitive on Ω (i.e. f is an Arrow social welfare function on Ω). Then so is the simple majority rule on Ω. Moreover, unless f is identical with simple majority voting, there exists some domain Ω' on which the majority rule is an Arrow social welfare function but f is not.

Maskin's result can be illustrated by comparing the majority rule with the Pareto extension rule. The latter says that for two alternatives x and y, x is socially at least as good as y iff y does not strictly Pareto-dominate x. We have already mentioned that for strict individual orderings only and for three alternatives a, b and c, let's say, value restriction (plus oddness) is necessary and sufficient for the simple majority rule to be an Arrow social welfare function. For three alternatives a, b and c, there are six strict orderings: abc, bca and cab (Latin Square 1), and cba, acb and bac (Latin Square 2). Sen's value restriction requires that one strict ordering be deleted from each Latin Square. The Pareto extension rule is transitive iff the property of – what Maskin calls – quasi-agreement is satisfied. The latter condition is stronger than value restriction. It is a domain restriction that demands that for all triples (x,y,z), there exists one alternative, say x, such that for all profiles (i) x is ranked higher than both y and z, or (ii) x is ranked lower than both y and z, or (iii) x is ranked between the other two alternatives. Thus, quasi-agreement requires that more than one strict ordering be deleted from each of the two Latin Squares.

What has just been shown for the Pareto extension rule has also been proved by Dasgupta and Maskin (1998) for the Borda count and for the 2/3-majority rule. For the Borda rule, for example, there is a clash between the neutrality property and any preference domain admitting more than quasi-agreement. Dasgupta and Maskin actually derived the latter results as well as an analogue to the above theorem for a situation where there is a continuum of voters (a large population). Individual indifference is ruled out as before and it is shown that the simple majority rule is 'maximally' robust. The authors have proved furthermore that if the anonymity condition is somewhat weakened, simple majority voting is no longer uniquely maximally robust. The class of weighted majority rules is maximally robust as well.

4.3 Maximal domains for strategy-proof voting procedures

In section 4.1, we briefly discussed Kalai and Muller's result on the existence of an n-person nondictatorial nonmanipulable voting procedure. In this section, we are interested in maximal domains for the existence of such rules. We start with a special class of rules that Barberà, Sonnenschein and Zhou (1991) have called voting by committees. It uses the structure of what we have defined in section 3.5 as (monotonic) simple games. Furthermore, Barberà, Sonnenschein and Zhou consider the case of a set of discrete alternatives – public goods or candidates to a club, let's say. Let $H = \{1,2,\ldots,h\}$ be the set of objects on which collective decisions are to be made. 2^H is the set of subsets of H, corresponding to $\Gamma \cup \{\emptyset\}$ in Kalai and Muller's notation. Again, Σ denotes the set of all strict preference orderings. Barberà, Sonnenschein and Zhou consider voting schemes that have each individual order the 2^h subsets of objects such that for each n-tuple of such orderings, an outcome of a set of objects is generated. Thus, a voting scheme f is a mapping from Σ^n to 2^H, where, again, $N = \{1,2,\ldots,n\}$ is the set of voters. A committee then is a pair $C = (N,\mathcal{W})$ with $\mathcal{W}$ being a nonempty set of winning coalitions and the ordered pair $(N,\mathcal{W})$ being a simple game. Let $P \in \Sigma$ be any strict preference on 2^H. $B(P)$ is defined as the best element of 2^H according to P, i.e. $B(P) = argmax(P,2^H)$.

According to the authors, a voting scheme $f : \Sigma^n \rightarrow 2^H$ is voting by committees, if for each object x, there exists a committee $C_x = (N, \mathcal{W}_x)$ such that for all profiles $(P_1, P_2, \ldots, P_n) \in \Sigma^n$, $x \in f(P_1, P_2, \ldots, P_n)$ iff $\{i | x \in B(P_i)\} \in \mathcal{W}_x$. Barberà, Sonnenschein and Zhou (1991) want a voting scheme to satisfy voter sovereignty which means that for each $A \subseteq H$, there exists a profile $(P_1, P_2, \ldots, P_n)$ such that $f(P_1, P_2, \ldots, P_n) = A$. Voter sovereignty forbids cases where some $A' \subseteq H$, for example, will *a priori* be barred from being chosen via f. The authors then introduce a domain constraint that leads to so-called separable preferences. They assume that a voter can evaluate each alternative separately from the other objects. In the case of an election of candidates to a club, for example, separability would disallow that a voter finds each of two candidates better than the combined choice of the two. For each $P \in \Sigma$, let $G(P) = \{x \in H | \{x\} P \emptyset\}$ be called the set of good objects. A preference relation $P \in \Sigma$ is said to be separable if for all $A \subseteq H$ and all $x \in A$, $(A \cup \{x\}) P A$ iff $x \in G(P)$. The set of all separable preferences is denoted by Σ^S. The authors note that additive representability implies separability (but not vice versa with more than two alternatives) and that whenever P is separable, $B(P)$ and $G(P)$ coincide: the best set is the set of all good objects.

The main result of Barberà, Sonnenschein and Zhou is a characterization of voting by committees on the domain of separable preferences.

Theorem 25 (Barberà, Sonnenschein and Zhou 1991). A voting scheme $f : (\Sigma^S)^n \rightarrow 2^H$ is strategy-proof on $(\Sigma^S)^n$ and satisfies voter sovereignty iff it is voting by committees.

Voting by quota where winning coalitions are determined by size only, can be characterized on domain Σ^S when anonymity and neutrality are imposed on the voting scheme f in addition to voter sovereignty and nonmanipulability.

Barberà, Sonnenschein and Zhou show furthermore that voting by committees cannot be strategy-proof on any larger domain, given that the power structure of the rule is 'nonextreme'.[7] Finally, the authors prove that even on the restricted domain of separable preferences, Pareto efficiency cannot be achieved. More precisely, for at least three objects, no efficient, strategy-proof and nondictatorial voting scheme exists on $(\Sigma^S)^n$.

We now want to consider the case of a perfectly divisible commodity to be allocated to agents. Sprumont (1991) showed that the so-called uniform rule is the only rule that satisfies strategy-proofness, anonymity and efficiency on the domain of single-peaked preferences. Ching (1994) strengthened this result by showing that anonymity can be weakened to what he called symmetry requiring that any two individuals with identical preferences receive amounts of the perfectly divisible commodity between which they are indifferent.

The question again is whether there is a domain larger than the domain of single-peaked preferences on which strategy-proof, efficient and symmetric voting rules exist. Ching and Serizawa (1998) were able to prove that one can extend single-peakedness to a single-plateaued domain. The voting rule then has to be adapted accordingly. While for single-peaked preferences the set of best elements is a singleton, single-plateaued preferences, in the case of a perfectly divisible commodity, allow the set of best elements to be a nondegenerate interval in the set of positive real numbers. The uniform rule has to be extended by considering the infimum and supremum of this interval. The maximal domain result then is

Theorem 26 (Ching and Serizawa 1998). The single-plateaued domain is the unique maximal domain including single-peaked preferences for a rule satisfying strategy-proofness, symmetry and efficiency.

Dummett and Farquharson (1961) realized that the Condorcet winner voting operation yields a social choice rule that is immune to any strategic manipulation by a voter. Moulin (1980) generalized this result by showing

---

[7] A committee is said to be nonextreme if it contains neither veto voters nor dummy voters.

that under the domain restriction of single-peaked preferences, the Condorcet winner is not the only strategy-proof voting mechanism. Every strategy-proof, efficient, and anonymous voting rule is obtained by adding $(n - 1)$ fixed ballots to the n ballots of the voters and then picking the median of this larger set of ballots. Thus, a generalized median voter system has been created. The $(n - 1)$ fixed ballots could come from some 'societal body' that can, in principle, always be overridden by a unanimous vote among the n individuals.

Given that the set of alternatives can be represented as points in a rectangular grid, Barberà, Massò and Neme (1999) have characterized the maximal sets of preferences under which generalized median voter schemes are strategy-proof. These mechanisms introduce some distribution of power among the voters. Some agents may never be able to influence the voting outcome at all (so-called dummies), some agents are decisive in the sense that they always dictate that the outcome be in a specific subset. Some agents are vetoers so that, if they wish, they can avoid some outcomes. In order to define precisely the version of single-peakedness the authors need to establish their possibility result, quite a bit of additional notation would be required. Loosely speaking, however, Barberà, Massò and Neme restrict the preferences of the individuals on two sets. One set is defined by the intersection of the range of the social choice function and a subset of alternatives on which the individual is not a dummy, the other set is defined by the intersection of the latter subset and the set of options left open to the other agents, when individual i declares preference P_i. All voters' preferences are required to be single-peaked with respect to the latter intersection. By permitting the existence of dummies in their median voter scheme, the authors were able to generalize an earlier result by Serizawa (1995).

4.4 Stability of group decision rules

In all the approaches of section 4.3, preference restrictions were imposed not only on sincere (or true) preference profiles but also on the set of preferences which the individuals express (ballot preferences). Imagine a society for which it is known *a priori* that all individual preferences satisfy a certain restriction, single-peakedness, let's say. Furthermore, every member in the society has this information. In these particular circumstances, confining the set of admissible ballots to the set of single-peaked preferences does not present a severe restriction. This is the argumentation which one finds in some of the contributions to this area and Ritz (1983) adds 'that once the type of a restricted domain an individual belongs to is known, any deviation will be recognized as blatantly untrue'. One could, however, object to this that even if the sincere preferences of the members of the society satisfy some reasonable restriction, this does not automatically mean that the strategic preferences of the individuals fulfil the *same type* of restriction.[8] Ritz's argument, however, still applies.

Zeckhauser (1973, p. 940) suggested that single-peakedness of sincere individual preferences alone is 'sufficient to eliminate any incentive for a voter to disguise his preferences' whenever the method of simple majority decision is used as the collective choice rule. Pattanaik (1976), however, provided a counter-example to this conjecture, showing that single-peakedness is not a sufficient condition for (what we shall call) 'stability' of sincere preference profiles.[9] The question then is under what restrictions of

---

[8] Note that much of social choice theory is purely static. Therefore, one cannot argue that at the moment when a certain voter submits a ballot, the preferences may be different from the earlier ones that satisfied some restriction.

[9] A similar result was established by Blin and Satterthwaite (1976). They used the majority rule with Borda completion and showed that if the true preferences are single-peaked but the ballot preferences unrestricted, strategy-proofness is not guaranteed. Single-peakedness of the set of admissible ballots is also required.

true preferences stability will result when the reported preferences are unrestricted.

Let X be a finite set of social states having at least three elements with S denoting a subset of X. S represents the set of feasible alternatives and we assume that $|S| \geq 3$. Furthermore, let Ω again denote a nonempty subset of Σ, the set of all strict preference orderings on X. The individual orderings in Ω are denoted by P_i, individual i's sincere ordering by P_i^*. Finally, let Γ be the set of subsets S of X with a cardinality of at least three for each of its elements.

Definition. A group decision function (GDF) is a function $F : \Sigma^n \times \Gamma \rightarrow 2^X \backslash \emptyset$ such that $F((P_1, \ldots, P_n), S) \subset S$.[10]

$F((P_1, \ldots, P_n), S)$ represents the set of chosen elements when S is the feasible set. If $F(\cdot)$ contains more than one element one can imagine that some random mechanism is applied in order to obtain a unique final outcome.

We now define some properties of a GDF.

Definition. Let F be a GDF, S be a subset of X which belongs to Γ and $(P_1, \ldots, P_n)$ and $(P'_1, \ldots, P'_n)$ two elements of Σ^n. $|N|$ again is the total number of voters.

(1) Binariness (B): If $\{x \in S \mid$ for all $y \in S, x \in F((P_1, \ldots, P_n), \{x, y\})\} \neq \emptyset$, then $F((P_1, \ldots, P_n), S) = \{x \in S \mid$ for all $y \in S, x \in F((P_1, \ldots, P_n), \{x, y\})\}$.

(2) Independence (I): If for all $x, y \in S$ and for all $i \in N, (xP_iy \leftrightarrow xP'_iy)$, then $F((P_1, \ldots, P_n), S) = F((P'_1, \ldots, P'_n), S)$.

(3) Neutrality (NT): Let σ be a one-to-one mapping from X to X such that for all $x, y \in X$ and for all $i \in N, (xP_iy \leftrightarrow \sigma(x)P'_i\sigma(y))$. Then for all $x \in S$, $[x \in F((P_1, \ldots, P_n), S) \leftrightarrow \sigma(x) \in F((P'_1, \ldots, P'_n), \sigma(S))]$, where $\sigma(S) = \{\sigma(x) \mid x \in S\}$.

(4) Monotonicity (M): Suppose for some $x \in S$, we have for all $a \in S$ and all $i \in N, (xP_ia \rightarrow xP'_ia)$ and for all $a, b \in S \backslash \{x\}$ and for all $i \in N, (aP_ib \leftrightarrow aP'_ib)$.

---

[10] The profile $(P_1, \ldots, P_n)$ stands for a vector of revealed strict preference orderings. These can be either sincere or nonsincere.

Then, $[F((P_1, \ldots, P_n), S) = \{x\}] \to [F((P'_1, \ldots, P'_n), S) = \{x\}]$ and $[x \in F((P_1, \ldots, P_n), S)] \to [x \in F((P'_1, \ldots, P'_n), S)]$.

(5) **Absence of Individual Vetoes** (*AV*): For all $x \in S$, if for all $y \in S \backslash \{x\}, |\{i \in N \mid xP_i y\}| \geq |N| - 1$, then $F((P_1, \ldots, P_n), S) = \{x\}$.

(6) **Weak Pareto Criterion** (*WP*): For all $x \in S$, if $\exists y \in S$ such that for all $i \in N, yP_i x$, then $x \notin F((P_1, \ldots, P_n), S)$.

(7) **Resoluteness** (*RS*): For all $x, y \in X, F((P_1, \ldots, P_n), \{x, y\})$ is a singleton.

We now introduce the individuals' rankings over alternative preference profiles. Given $S \in \Gamma, T_j^S$ represents a binary relation on Σ^n, indicating individual j's ranking over alternative profiles. V_j^S and J_j^S are the antisymmetric and symmetric components of T_j^S. Following Pattanaik (1973), it will be assumed that in ranking alternative profiles $(P_1, \ldots, P_n)$ and $(P'_1, \ldots, P'_n)$, each voter follows a maximin rule defined as follows:

For any $S' \subset S$, let $\min(S', P_i^*) = \{x \mid x \in S' \land$ for all $y \in S', yP_i^* x\}$. Let $M_1^i = \min(S', P_i^*)$ and for all integers $k > 1$, let $M_k^i = \min(S' \backslash M_1^i \backslash M_2^i \backslash \ldots \backslash M_{k-1}^i)$.

Definition. Let $S \in \Gamma$ and $(P_1, \ldots, P_n), (P'_1, \ldots, P'_n) \in \Sigma^n$. Furthermore, $z = F((P_1, \ldots, P_n), S)$ and $z' = F((P'_1, \ldots, P'_n), S)$. An individual j is said to follow a maximin rule if both of the following conditions hold:

(i) $(P_1, \ldots, P_n) J_j^S (P'_1, \ldots, P'_n)$, if $z = z'$;

(ii) $(P_1, \ldots, P_n) V_j^S (P'_1, \ldots, P'_n)$, if there exists a positive integer k such that for all integers $t(0 < t < k), M_t^j(z) = M_t^j(z')$ and either (for some $x, y \in S, M_k^j(z) = \{x\}$ and $M_k^j(z') = \{y\}$ and $xP_j^* y)$ or $(M_k^j(z) \neq \emptyset$ and $M_k^j(z') = \emptyset)$.

Under this maximin rule an individual ranks two preference profiles $(P_1, \ldots, P_n)$ and $(P'_1, \ldots, P'_n)$ according to his sincere preferences, where the minima of the sets of outcomes z and z' are compared.[11]

[11] More details on this type of behaviour can be found in Pattanaik (1973, 1978).

We now define the notion of stability[12] of a preference profile and also that of a *GDF*.

Definition. Given $S \in \Gamma, (P_1, \ldots, P_n) \in \Sigma^n$ is stable with respect to S if there does not exist a profile $(P'_1, \ldots, P'_n) \in \Sigma^n$ and a coalition $G \subset N$ such that

(1) for all $i \in N \backslash G, P'_i = P_i$;
(2) for some $i \in G, P'_i \neq P_i$;
(3) for all $i \in G, (P'_1, \ldots, P'_n) V^S_i (P_1, \ldots, P_n)$.

A *GDF* is stable with respect to S if every sincere profile $(P^*_1, \ldots, P^*_n)$ is stable with respect to S. A *GDF* is stable if it is stable for every $S \in \Gamma$.

For all $S \in \Gamma$ and for all $\Omega \subset \Sigma$, we define $S^*_\Omega = \{x \in S \mid \not\exists y \in S$ such that for all $P_i \in \Omega, y P_i x\}$. S^*_Ω thus represents the set of Pareto-optimal elements in S, given Ω.

Definition (Sengupta and Dutta 1979). Given $S \in \Gamma$, a set of strict orderings $\Omega \subset \Sigma$ satisfies the property of Restricted Pareto Optimality (*RPO*) over S iff $|S^*_\Omega| \leq 2$.

We are now able to state the following result.

Theorem 27 (Sengupta and Dutta 1979). Let F satisfy B, I, NT, M, AV and WP but violate RS. Then F is stable iff every set of sincere strict preference orderings satisfies *RPO* over S.

Unfortunately, condition *RPO* is very stringent. It requires that in a set of feasible alternatives, the number of Pareto–optimal alternatives is at most two. This means that in order to obtain stability, a high degree of similarity among the voters' sincere preference orderings is required. Over each triple of alternatives in the feasible set, at least one alternative is Pareto-dominated. Note again that the theorem above imposes restrictions on the configurations of sincere orderings and not on the configurations of orderings which the individuals express.

---

[12] The game-theoretic origin of this concept can be traced back to Nash (1951), Shubik (1959) and Farquharson (1969).

Dutta (1977) has generalized the above result. He showed that a necessary and sufficient condition for any preference profile (sincere or nonsincere) to be stable is that every permissible set of orderings satisfies *RPO* over *S*. Furthermore, he proved that if every individual's sincere preferences are strict and satisfy property *RPO*, the only stable set of outcomes is the set of outcomes that corresponds to the sincere situation. This latter result is quite appealing from an ethical point of view. Suppose that there exists some nonsincere situation which is also stable. Then, if some individuals are not voting sincerely, the resulting outcomes will form a subset of the set corresponding to the sincere situation. No outcome which is considered nonoptimal under the sincere orderings can be selected.

Coming back to the conjecture of Zeckhauser mentioned at the beginning of this section, the condition of single-peakedness of sincere preference orderings actually does have some bearing on the issue of stability. Pattanaik (1976, 1978, p. 141) demonstrated that if the sincere profile satisfies the property of weak single-peakedness (which is essentially equivalent to not-worst value restriction) and if, in addition, there is a unique outcome *x*, let's say, for the sincere preference profile, then no coalition *G*, by voting strategically, will find it possible to bring about another unique outcome which each member of *G* prefers to *x* on the basis of the sincere ordering. However, this result does not necessarily carry over to the case where the sets of chosen elements are no longer singletons (for another result involving the property of strict single-peakedness, i.e. 'no plateau at the top', see Pattanaik 1978, pp. 143–6).

For the case of unique social outcomes (the social decision rule satisfies the property of resoluteness), Dutta (1980) has formulated a necessary and sufficient condition for stability.[13]

---

[13] In that paper the author used a somewhat different terminology. He called 'Type I-consistency' what we have called 'stability'.

Definition. Weak Condition of Reward for Pairwise Optimality (*WRPO*).

Let F be a group decision rule, S be a subset of X belonging to Γ and $(P_1, \ldots, P_n) \in \Omega^n$. For all $x \in S$, if for all $y \in S \backslash \{x\}, \{x\} = F((P_1, \ldots, P_n), \{x, y\})$, then $\{x\} = F((P_1, \ldots, P_n), S)$.

The condition of binariness B, defined above, implies property *WRPO*. The result is

Theorem 28 (Dutta 1980). Let F satisfy *WRPO,I,NT,M, AV* and *RS*. Then F is stable iff the set of sincere strict preference orderings satisfies condition *VR* over every triple of alternatives in S.

Note that since every individual sincere ordering is assumed to be strict, property *RPO* implies *VR*. Thus the domain of F appears to be larger under theorem 28 than under Sengupta and Dutta's theorem 27. Nevertheless, the two results are logically independent of each other.

CHAPTER 5

RESTRICTIONS ON THE DISTRIBUTION OF INDIVIDUALS' PREFERENCES

A common feature of the restrictions on individual preference relations presented in chapter 3 was that certain individual preferences were not allowed to occur at all (as in the case of Inada's dichotomous preferences) or were excluded in the presence of other preference relations (as, for example, in the case of Sen and Pattanaik's extremal restriction). The approach that we shall follow in the present section is to admit all logically possible individual orderings but to look for conditions on the distribution of voters' preferences such that a consistent (transitive, quasi-transitive or acyclic) majority decision is guaranteed.

5.1 The majority decision rule

5.1.1 Conditions on the distribution of preferences in the original profile

Definition. For any triple of alternatives x,y,z: (i) x is strictly best (semi-strictly best) in the aggregate sense (i.e. collectively) if xPy and xPz (either $xPy \wedge xRz \vee xRy \wedge xPz$); (ii) x is strictly worst (semi-strictly worst) in the aggregate sense if yPx and zPx (either $yPx \wedge zRx \vee yRx \wedge zPx$); (iii) there is total indifference in the aggregate sense over the triple if xIy, yIz, and xIz.

Definition. The Extended Condorcet Condition (*ECC*) is satisfied iff for every triple of alternatives (x,y,z) there is at least one issue which is strictly best or strictly worst in the aggregate sense, or the triple of alternatives is totally indifferent in the aggregate sense.

Restrictions on the distribution of individuals' preferences

Bowman and Colantoni (1972) have proved the following theorem for the existence of a transitive social relation.

Theorem 29 (Bowman and Colantoni 1972). Iff condition *ECC* is satisfied for every triple of alternatives, the collective preference relation is transitive under the majority decision rule.

As we are interested to characterize those distributions of voters' preferences that ensure collective transitivity, we may find it helpful to number the 13 logically possible individual orderings of a triple (x,y,z) in the following way:

(1) xP_iyP_iz (7) xP_iyI_iz
(2) xP_izP_iy (8) yP_ixI_iz
(3) yP_ixP_iz (9) zP_ixI_iy
(4) yP_izP_ix (10) xI_iyP_iz
(5) zP_ixP_iy (11) xI_izP_iy
(6) zP_iyP_ix (12) zI_iyP_ix
(13) xI_iyI_iz.

In what follows n_i denotes the number of voters who have preference ordering i in the above scheme. The fulfilment of condition *ECC* is equivalent to finding a solution to the following system of linear inequalities as stated in the next theorem.

Theorem 30 (Bowman and Colantoni 1972).[1] A triple (x,y,z) satisfies condition *ECC* iff for the three equations

(i) $n_1 + n_2 + n_5 + n_7 + n_{11}[Q_1]n_3 + n_4 + n_6 + n_8 + n_{12}$
                                      (x versus y),

(ii) $n_1 + n_2 + n_3 + n_7 + n_{10}[Q_2]n_4 + n_5 + n_6 + n_9 + n_{12}$
                                      (x versus z),

(iii) $n_1 + n_3 + n_4 + n_8 + n_{10}[Q_3]n_2 + n_5 + n_6 + n_9 + n_{11}$
                                      (y versus z),

---

[1] In an unpublished paper Saposnik (n.d.) has derived a theorem along the same lines. His result is, however, more general in so far as no assumptions whatever are made with respect to completeness or any kind of consistency of the underlying individual preference relations (see also Gaertner 1979, who discusses Saposnik's approach).

(where $[Q_i]$ is the relation $'<'$, $'='$, or $'>'$) the set of relation-ships $(Q = (Q_1, Q_2, Q_3)$ has one of the following forms

(a) $Q = (>, >, Q_3)$, x strictly best,
(b) $Q = (<, <, Q_3)$, x strictly worst,
(c) $Q = (<, Q_2, >)$, y strictly best,
(d) $Q = (>, Q_2, <)$, y strictly worst,
(e) $Q = (Q_1, <, <)$, z strictly best,
(f) $Q = (Q_1, >, >)$, z strictly worst,
(g) $Q = (=, =, =)$,   total indifference.

Clearly there is a multitude of distributions of voters' preferences that satisfy the requirement of theorem 30. All the domain restriction conditions which are sufficient for the existence of a social ordering obviously must fulfil the requirement.[2] As long as one is primarily interested in what we wish to call qualitative conditions specifying structural properties of the underlying preference profile (such as, e.g. single-peakedness or extremal restriction), theorem 30 is not very helpful since it does not provide such qualitative character-izations. Note that the requirement of theorem 30 is satisfied by any profile that gives rise to a transitive social relation. Consider, for example, the case where the number of voters who have preference ordering 3, let's say, is strictly larger than the total number of voters having any of the other orderings, i.e.

$$n_3 > \sum_{\substack{i=1 \\ i \neq 3}}^{13} n_i.$$

Or the case where $n_1 - n_6 > n_4 + n_5, n_2, n_3, n_7$ and n_{13} being any positive integers, and

$$\sum_{i=8}^{12} n_i = 0.$$

---

[2] See Bowman and Colantoni (1972) for a proof of this statement.

Bowman and Colantoni (1974) have shown a way to give a general characterization of all those distributions of individual preferences that yield a social ordering. Their point of departure is an immediate consequence of theorem 30 above.

Corollary (Bowman and Colantoni 1972). Intransitivity occurs in a triple (x,y,z) iff the equations of theorem 30 have $Q = (\geq, \leq, \geq)$ or $Q = (\leq, \geq, \leq)$ with at least one strict inequality in either set.[3]

Clearly the corollary could be used to investigate the existence of transitivity with respect to any given distribution of individual voters. This would imply nothing else but counting the votes over each pair of social alternatives. However, the corollary can also be used for stating two systems of inequalities such that the non-existence of a solution to each of these is equivalent to the existence of social transitivity. The lack of a solution to these sets of inequalities can be associated with the existence of a solution to another set of inequalities by an application of the theorem of the alternative (cf. Tucker 1956; Gale 1960). Therefore, an equivalence is manifested between transitive majority decisions and the existence of a (positive) solution to a certain set of linear inequalities (see pp. 491–3 in Bowman and Colantoni 1974, theorem 5 in particular).[4]

This novel approach makes it possible for the authors to present an alternative proof of the Sen and Pattanaik case where the individual preference orderings satisfy the extremal restriction condition. However, more compli-

---

[3] We should like to mention that Nicholson (1965) established a necessary and sufficient condition for social intransitivity for the situation of 3 voters and 3 alternatives with each voter having a strict preference ordering. When generalizing this result to the case where weak individual orderings are also admitted Nicholson arrived at the condition in the corollary.

[4] We abstain from giving a precise statement of Bowman and Colantoni's theorem 5 as this would compel us to introduce quite a bit of additional notation. See also Bowman and Colantoni (1973).

cated distributions of voters' preferences with no *a priori* exclusion seem tractable now. One sufficient condition for transitivity, a rather trivial one, has already been mentioned: the case where one strict ordering strictly outnumbers (dominates) all the other orderings taken together. The following result appears to be much more interesting.

Theorem 31 (Bowman and Colantoni 1974). A sufficient condition for collective transitivity over a triple of alternatives under the majority rule is that the fraction of individuals who rate one particular alternative semi-strictly best (semi-strictly worst) in their individual orderings is greater than 3/4.

If there are more than three alternatives, this condition has to hold with respect to every triple. Still other specifications of the n_i's sufficient for generating social transitivity should be derivable.

Let us now consider distributions of individuals on the plane or on higher-dimensional spaces. In his examination of Arrow's impossibility result Tullock (1967) provided an example where each individual i is characterized by a point a_i in the space $\mathbb{R}^2$ such that for every x and y in X, x is at least as good as y iff the distance between x and a_i is not greater than the distance between y and a_i. The distribution of individuals among preferences can then be described by a probability distribution on the plane. In Tullock's example the individuals, i.e. the best points a_i, are uniformly distributed over a rectangle with centre a^*. It is not difficult to show that the simple majority rule must then be transitive.

Grandmont (1978) who began his analysis with Tullock's example established a theorem which – roughly speaking – says that if the preference relations of the members of society are 'nicely' distributed around some relation R_a^*, then the method of majority decision selects a relation which coincides with R_a^*. Grandmont starts out by considering a family of relations $(R_a)_{a\in A}$, defined on a set of alternatives X, which is indexed by a point a running over a convex subset A of an arbitrary Euclidean

Restrictions on the distribution of individuals' preferences

space $\mathbb{R}^n$. The family $(R_a)_{a \in A}$ is required to have a continuity property (C.1) and a 'betweenness' property (C.2).[5]

(C.1) For every x and y in X, the set $\{a \in A \mid xR_a y\}$ is closed in A.

(C.2) For every a' and a'' in $A, R_a \in (R_{a'}, R_{a''})$ whenever $a = \lambda a' + (1 - \lambda)a''$, where $\lambda \in (0,1)$.

$R_a \in (R_{a'}, R_{a''})$ has the 'betweenness' property saying that for any two points a' and a'', relation R_a must lie between the relations $R_{a'}$ and $R_{a''}$ (cf. pp. 320–2 in Grandmont 1978). Grandmont shows that a family of relations $(R_a)_{a \in A}$, where A is an open convex subset of $\mathbb{R}^n$, satisfies (C.1) and (C.2) iff for every x and y in X, one of the following conditions holds: (1) either $xP_a y$ for all a, or $xI_a y$ for all a, or $yP_a x$ for all a; (2) there exists q in $\mathbb{R}^n$, $q \neq 0$, and a real number c such that $qa > c$ when $xP_a y, qa = c$ when $xI_a y$, and $qa < c$ when $yP_a x$.

We can now define a probability distribution on A and a majority relation based on this distribution. Consider the class of societies whose individuals have preferences which belong to $(R_a)_{a \in A}$, with A as defined, satisfying properties (C.1) and (C.2). Any society in this class can be characterized by a probability distribution ν on A. For given alternatives x and y in X, $\nu(xR_a y)$ represents the proportion of voters having $xR_a y$. The majority relation R^M is then defined as $xR^M y$ iff $\nu(xR_a y) \geq \nu(yR_a x)$.

For any hyperplane H in $\mathbb{R}^n$, let A' and A'' denote the intersections of A with the two closed half-spaces determined by H. Consider x and y, and let H be the unique hyperplane of equation $qa = c$ associated to x and y due to condition (2) above. Let $\mathcal{H}$ be the family of such hyperplanes which is generated when x and y vary in X. Now the majority relation R^M coincides with R_{a^*} for some a^* in A iff:

(M) For every H in $\mathcal{H}, \nu(A') \geq \nu(A'')$ iff $a^* \in A'$.

[5] Note that in Grandmont's approach it is the set of individuals which has a topological structure and not (necessarily) the set of social states X.

A stronger condition is obtained by requiring that the property stated in (M) be valid for every hyperplane H of $\mathbb{R}^n$, not only for those of $\mathcal{H}$:

(M.1) There exists a^* in A such that for every hyperplane H of $\mathbb{R}^n$, $v(A') = v(A'')$ iff $a^* \in H$.

Grandmont established the following result.

Theorem 32 (Grandmont 1978). Let $(R_a)_{a \in A}$ be a family of relations on a set of alternatives X, where A is open and convex in $\mathbb{R}^n$, which satisfies (C.1) and (C.2). Then for any probability distribution v on A which satisfies (M.1), the majority relation R^M coincides with R_{a^*}.

Note that the result in the theorem also holds when the relations of the family $(R_a)_{a \in A}$ are not transitive. If one considers individual orderings only, as in Tullock's example, the majority relation R^M is transitive 'automatically'. The majority relation can be identified with a representative member of the family, a^*. The weaker condition (M) can be used when one-dimensional families of relations are studied. Grandmont shows (1) that when $(R_a)_{a \in A}$ is a family of transitive preference relations on a set X satisfying (C.1) and (C.2), where A is an open interval of the real line, then preferences are single-peaked or single-caved; (2) when $(R_a)_{a \in A}$ is a one-dimensional family of relations and society comprises an odd number of voters, then for every triple of alternatives, there is an a^* in A such that the majority relation coincides with R_{a^*} on that triple. This shows that the well-known possibility theorem for single-peaked (or single-caved) preferences is just a special case within a more general framework.

Saposnik (1975b) has presented a sufficient condition for transitivity where a distributional requirement is made only with respect to the set of strict individual orderings. According to his terminology, for any ordered triple (x,y,z) of alternatives the 'clockwise cycle' of individual orderings is defined to be

$$(1) \quad xP_iyP_iz$$
$$(4) \quad yP_izP_ix$$
$$(5) \quad zP_ixP_iy,$$

and the 'counter-clockwise cycle' of individual rankings is similarly defined as

$$(6) \quad zP_iyP_ix$$
$$(2) \quad xP_izP_iy$$
$$(3) \quad yP_ixP_iz.$$

'Cyclical balance' of the voters' preference profile is then given iff there is the same number of individual orderings constituting the clockwise cycle and the counter-clockwise cycle, i.e. $n_1 + n_4 + n_5 = n_2 + n_3 + n_6$.
Saposnik's result is

Theorem 33 (Saposnik 1975b). Under the majority decision rule the social preference relation is transitive if the individual preference relations are cyclically balanced.

The domain of cyclically balanced preferences may appear rather small but Saposnik observed that in his approach the distribution of voters over the subset of orderings with at least one indifference has no bearing on the transitivity issue. Gaertner and Heinecke (1977) have proved that cyclical balance is a rather unique property in the sense that it is not only sufficient but also necessary for this result to hold.[6]

Saposnik also showed that his result can be generalized to the case of quasi-transitive individual rankings.

---

[6] Gaertner and Heinecke have shown in addition that Saposnik's theorem and Inada's result on dichotomous preferences follow from each other if certain reductions are introduced that transform an originally given preference profile into a reduced set of preference orderings (see subsection 5.1.2 below). More concretely, a preference profile that satisfies Saposnik's condition can be reduced either to a set containing only dichotomous preferences or to an empty set; the latter yields complete social indifference among the alternatives involved.

Kaneko (1975) presented a necessary and sufficient condition[7] for transitive majority decisions which relies on the assumption that over a given triple of alternatives x,y,z all logically possible strict orderings have to occur at least once. This requirement is interesting in so far as it is the very opposite to the exclusion-type domain restriction conditions in chapter 3. Before stating Kaneko's results, a few definitions have to be introduced.

For every distinct three alternatives x,y,z we define $W^m(x,y,z)$ and $k^m(x,y,z)$ by

$$W^m(x,y,z) = \{\{i \in N \mid aR_ib\} \mid aPb; a,b \in (x,y,z)\},$$
$$k^m(x,y,z) = \{(a,b) \mid aPb; a,b \in (x,y,z)\}.$$

We can interpret $W^m(x,y,z)$ as the collection of winning groups of voters for all pairs $a,b \in (x,y,z)$ under the majority decision rule; $k^m(x,y,z)$ denotes the set of pairs of alternatives between which a strict social preference exists under the majority rule.

Kaneko writes

$$W^m(x,y,z) = \{S\} \qquad \text{if} \quad \#(W^m(x,y,z)) = 1$$
$$= \{S,T\} \qquad \text{if} \quad \#(W^m(x,y,z)) = 2$$
$$= \{S,T,V\} \qquad \text{if} \quad \#(W^m(x,y,z)) = 3.$$

The #-sign stands for cardinality. $U^m(x,y,z)$ is defined by

$$U^m(x,y,z) = \emptyset \qquad \text{if} \quad \#(W^m(x,y,z)) \leq 1$$
$$= S \cup T \qquad \text{if} \quad \#(W^m(x,y,z)) = 2$$
$$= (S \cap T) \cup (T \cap V)$$
$$\cup (V \cap S) \qquad \text{if} \quad \#(W^m(x,y,z)) = 3.$$

Now we can formulate

---

[7] In order to explain Kaneko's concept of necessary condition, we use a quotation from the author himself (p. 385): 'If a profile of individual preference orderings makes the social preference transitive, then the profile satisfies the condition, where the number and names of individuals are fixed'. See also n.1 at the beginning of chapter 3 and Gaertner (1979, pp. 92–3, 108–11).

Theorem 34 (Kaneko 1975). Assume that for all distinct $x,y,z \in X$ there are individuals $i_1,i_2,\ldots,i_6 \in N$ such that

$$
\begin{aligned}
&i_1 : xP_iyP_iz \qquad &&i_6 : zP_iyP_ix \\
&i_4 : yP_izP_ix \qquad &&i_2 : xP_izP_iy \qquad (K^*) \\
&i_5 : zP_ixP_iy \qquad &&i_3 : yP_ixP_iz.
\end{aligned}
$$

Then the strict social preference relation P given by the majority rule is transitive iff for all distinct $x,y,z \in X$, the following condition (K^{**}) holds:

$$
\begin{aligned}
&&(xR_iy \quad \text{or} \quad xR_iz \qquad &\forall i \in U^m(x,y,z)) \\
\text{or} \quad &&(yR_ix \quad \text{or} \quad yR_iz \qquad &\forall i \in U^m(x,y,z)) \\
\text{or} \quad &&(zR_ix \quad \text{or} \quad zR_iy \qquad &\forall i \in U^m(x,y,z)) \qquad (K^{**}) \\
\text{or} \quad &&(yR_ix \quad \text{or} \quad zR_ix \qquad &\forall i \in U^m(x,y,z)) \\
\text{or} \quad &&(xR_iy \quad \text{or} \quad zR_iy \qquad &\forall i \in U^m(x,y,z)) \\
\text{or} \quad &&(xR_iz \quad \text{or} \quad yR_iz \qquad &\forall i \in U^m(x,y,z)).
\end{aligned}
$$

A couple of comments are now in order. Note first that $W^m(x,y,z)$ contains at most three coalitions or winning groups. Secondly, condition (K^{**}) formulates preference restrictions for the individuals in $U^m(x,y,z)$. So if the number of winning groups for all pairs of a given triple (x,y,z) is equal to one (i.e. there is one coalition that determines the social preferences over the triple), there is no domain restriction at all. The preferences of the individuals outside the coalition just do not matter. If there are two winning groups, then the restriction is imposed on the preferences of individuals who belong to at least one winning group. If there are three winning groups, then (K^{**}) formulates restrictions on the preferences of persons who belong to at least two winning groups. If the restrictions on $U^m(x,y,z)$ had been imposed on the set of all voters, the upper half and the lower half of (K^{**}) would have been called 'not strictly worst' and 'not strictly best' value restrictions, respectively (see subsection 3.5.1 above).

In order to illustrate Kaneko's result, consider the following two examples where we state preferences in the way it is done in (K^*):

Example 1.

$$4 : xP_iyP_iz\ (S) \qquad 1 : zP_iyP_ix\ (S')$$
$$1 : yP_izP_ix\ (T) \qquad 4 : xP_izP_iy\ (T')$$
$$4 : zP_ixP_iy\ (V) \qquad 1 : yP_ixP_iz\ (V').$$

There is a group of four individuals that we call group S, having the preference xP_iyP_iz. There is a group containing just one individual that we call group T, having the preference yP_izP_ix, etc. Obviously, the cardinality of $W^m(x,y,z)$ is equal to 3 and we have $U^m(x,y,z) = (S \cap V) \cup (V \cap T') \cup (S \cap T')$. One can easily check that $U^m(x,y,z)$ satisfies (K^{**}): $\forall i \in U^m(x,y,z)$ we have xR_iy or zR_iy. We obtain $xPzPy$ as the social preference.

Example 2.

$$4 : xP_iyP_iz\ (S) \qquad 1 : zP_iyP_ix\ (S')$$
$$4 : yP_izP_ix\ (T) \qquad 1 : xP_izP_iy\ (T')$$
$$4 : zP_ixP_iy\ (V) \qquad 1 : yP_ixP_iz\ (V').$$

Again, $\#(W^m(x,y,z)) = 3$. For $U^m(x,y,z)$ we obtain $U^m(x,y,z) = (S \cap V) \cup (V \cap T) \cup (T \cap S)$, but none of the restrictions under (K^{**}) is satisfied. We get the strict preference cycle $xPyPzPx$.

We noted before that (K^*) excludes no strict individual preference ordering of the set of all logically possible orderings over a triple (x,y,z). This, however, means that (K^*) violates the conditions of 'not strictly worst' and 'not strictly best' value restrictions. Also, (K^*) is not compatible with the notion of necessary condition as defined at the beginning of chapter 3. Kaneko argues that (K^*) will usually be satisfied for large societies where the chances that one particular ordering does not occur may be quite small.

86

A necessary and sufficient condition for transitivity of the social relation R under the majority rule is given by

Theorem 35 (Kaneko 1975). Under assumption (K*) of theorem 34, the social preference relation R, determined by the method of majority decision, is transitive iff for all distinct $x,y,z \in X$, (K**) of theorem 34 holds and furthermore $\#(k^m(x,y,z)) \neq 1$.

A final point that we would like to mention is that in some sense Kaneko's theorems represent an *ex post* verification (and explanation) of the existence or nonexistence of social transitivity. In other words: the characterization of preference profiles that yield transitive majority decisions can be given only after the structure of $U^m(x,y,z)$ has been determined. This structure, however, is highly sensitive to changes in the original preference profile and can be ascertained only *after* having counted all individual votes. It may help to clarify this point further by having another brief look at Saposnik's theorem above. Cyclical balance is a structural condition of the underlying profile in the sense that just by checking whether the individual orderings satisfy the condition, and not by counting all votes over each pair of alternatives, one can infer whether social transitivity is given or not. The set of winning groups in Kaneko's approach cannot be determined this way.

5.1.2 Conditions on the distribution of preferences in the reduced profile

Under the method of majority decision all those voters who are indifferent between every pair of alternatives out of a given set have no influence on the formation of the collective preference relation. Therefore, there are good reasons to disregard these unconcerned individuals. This (trivial) observation can immediately be extended to other cases. Consider a preference profile where five individuals, let's say, have the ordering yP_izP_ix and five other individuals have the opposite ordering xP_izP_iy. Obviously, these

10 voters can be excluded from further analysis under simple majority decisions.

Independent from each other, Slutsky (1975, 1977), Gaertner (1977, 1988) and Gaertner and Heinecke (1978) have taken this observation as their point of departure to construct new (imaginary) societies which, under majority voting, are equivalent to originally given societies but are more 'tractable' owing to a simplified preference profile. Gaertner (1988) uses a concept of 'preference proximity' within a given set of individual orderings to state a necessary and sufficient condition for collective transitivity under the method of majority decision. This notion of proximity is characterized by 'a path of binary inversions' of adjacent alternatives in the reduced preference profile of a given society.

Let $N(xP_iy)$ denote the number of voters for whom xP_iy as before. The vector $(N(xP_iy) - N(yP_ix), N(xP_iz) - N(zP_ix),$ $N(yP_iz) - N(zP_iy))$ will be called the majority vector of the underlying preference profile Π. Under the method of majority decision the majority vector determines the collective preference relation R. Clearly, two preference profiles characterized by the same majority vector yield the same social preference relation. For our analysis, these two profiles will be considered as equivalent.

In the following it proves very useful to come back to Saposnik's notion of clockwise and counter-clockwise cycles and define the following cycles (or groups) of individual orderings for a given triple (x,y,z):

C^+ :	C^- :
type 1: xR_iyR_iz	type 1: zR_iyR_ix
type 2: yR_izR_ix	type 2: xR_izR_iy
type 3: zR_ixR_iy.	type 3: yR_ixR_iz.

We shall call C^+ and C^- the clockwise and the counter-clockwise R-cycle, respectively. The corresponding P-cycles of strict preference are generated from C^+ and C^- by substituting $P - P$ orderings for $R - R$ orderings everywhere. Similarly, the $P - I$ cycle (with one strict preference and one indifference in each individual ordering) and the

Restrictions on the distribution of individuals' preferences

$I - P$ cycle (indifference first, then strict preference) are obtained from C^+ and C^- by replacing the $R - R$ orderings everywhere by $P - I$ orderings and $I - P$ orderings, respectively. Note that for the reduction procedure proposed in the sequel, it does not matter whether a particular $I - P$ ordering, for example, is assigned to C^+ or to C^- (but it should, of course, be assigned only once). More concretely, individual i's weak ordering xI_iyP_iz can either be assigned to type 1 of C^+ or to type 3 of C^-.

Consider a preference profile consisting of only two individual orderings. We wish to say that these two orderings are inverse to each other if the majority vector of this profile is $(0,0,0)$. The orderings xP_iyP_iz and zP_jyP_jx with $i, j \in N$, for example, yield the majority vector $(0,0,0)$; so do the orderings xP_iyI_iz and zI_jyP_jx. In both cases, therefore, we say that the individual orderings are inverse.[8]

More interestingly, the majority vector $(0,0,0)$ is also obtained in the situation of a complete $P - I$ cycle; by this we mean a $P - I$ cycle where each of the three possible $P - I$ orderings is held by exactly one individual. The same result is, of course, obtained for a complete $I - P$ cycle.

As already stated in subsection 5.1.1 above, we are primarily interested in qualitative or structural properties, and this should also refer to reduced preference profiles. Consequently, the property of dominance is of no great interest to us (it is studied additionally in Slutsky's contributions). We shall therefore use the concept of necessity in the sense in which it was used by Inada, Pattanaik, Sen and others who were interested in structural properties of *original* preference profiles, focusing only on types of permissible preference orderings and not on numbers of individuals holding the various orderings.

We now propose to transform the preference profile Π of a given (original) society into another more tractable one,

---

[8] The idea to eliminate inverse preference orderings of equal numbers has also been taken up by Feld and Grofman (1986). They use the term 'net preference' for the outcome of a procedure where pairs of inverse strict orderings are deleted.

denoted Π^*. This process of simplification (reduction procedure) is performed by eliminating and/or combining certain orderings (or sets of orderings) of Π in such a way that the majority vector is left unchanged, the number of types of orderings in Π^*, however, being considerably diminished (if a reduction is at all possible). The following types of simplifications will be distinguished:

ρ_1: Elimination of all pairs of individual $P - I$ and $I - P$ orderings which are inverse to each other.

ρ_2: Elimination of all complete $P - I$ cycles and $I - P$ cycles.

ρ_3: Transformation of all remaining individual $P - I$ orderings and $I - P$ orderings into strict preference orderings $P - P$. As an example, the ordering xP_izI_iy, which occurs n_i-times, let's say, is transformed into the two strict orderings $xPzPy$ and $xPyPz$, each occurring $\frac{n_i}{2}$-times. Analogously, the ordering yI_jxP_jz, which occurs, let's say, n_j-times, will be transformed into $yPxPz$ and $xPyPz$, each occurring $\frac{n_j}{2}$-times.[9]

ρ_4: Elimination of all pairs of individual strict orderings which are inverse to each other.

We wish to postulate that all four types of reductions are always performed in the given order. The preference profile Π of an original society is said to have obtained its reduced equivalent strict preference profile Π^* iff all four reductions have been executed, i.e. if

$$\rho_i(\Pi^*) = \Pi^*, i \in \{1,2,3,4\}.$$

Let $N_j(K_j)$ be the number of individuals in Π^* who hold the type-j ordering of $C^+(C^-)$ in its strict form $P - P$. Then profile Π^* is characterized by the following simple property:

---

[9] Of course, $\frac{n_i}{2}$ and $\frac{n_j}{2}$ may no longer be integers. This, however, does not matter (in our imaginary society). What matters in binary majority comparisons is whether $\frac{n_i}{2}$, let's say, is at least as large as or smaller than some other number, be it $\frac{n_j}{2}$ or some n_k.

Restrictions on the distribution of individuals' preferences

$$\forall j \in \{1, 2, 3\} : N_j > O \to K_j = O.$$

It is now easy to show that the logically possible set of reduced profiles Π^* comprises exactly six different elements. These are[10]:

$\Pi^*_{0,0}$: no strict orderings at all;
$\Pi^*_{1,0}$: strict individual orderings of one type occur;
$\Pi^*_{2,0}$: strict individual orderings of two types occur;
$\Pi^*_{3,0}$: strict individual orderings of all three types occur;
$\Pi^*_{1,1}$: strict orderings of one type from C^+ and one type from C^- occur;
$\Pi^*_{2,1}$: strict orderings of two types from C^+ and one type from C^- occur.

As already indicated we wish to work with a notion of nearness or proximity of individual preferences which uses the idea of binary inversions of adjacent alternatives. Given any set of individual orderings making up society's preference profile, we construct the reduced equivalent strict preference profile and ask whether it is possible to find a path which links all remaining orderings in the following sense: Moving from any one type of ordering to the next requires one and only one inversion of adjacent alternatives. Repeating this operation step by step leads from the first picked to the last type of individual orderings, thus completing the reduced preference profile. Let us depict the foregoing by means of the following example.

Assume that the original preference profile Π has

within type 1 of C^+: one person saying xP_iyP_iz, two persons with xI_iyP_iz and three persons holding xP_iyI_iz;
within type 2 of C^+: one person with yP_izP_ix and two with yI_izP_ix;

[10] It can easily be shown that for our purposes we need not distinguish between profiles Π^* which have the property of being identical up to a permutation of alternatives. This means that henceforth we need not, for example, look at $\Pi^*_{0,2}$ and $\Pi^*_{1,2}$ when we have already considered $\Pi^*_{2,0}$ and $\Pi^*_{2,1}$.

within type 3 of C^+: one person with zP_ixP_iy and two with zI_ixP_iy;
within type 1 of C^-: one person holding zP_iyP_ix.

Reduction ρ_2 eliminates two complete $I - P$ cycles. According to ρ_3, the three weak orderings xP_iyI_iz are transformed into $1\frac{1}{2}$ having xP_iyP_iz and $1\frac{1}{2}$ having xP_izP_iy. Reduction ρ_4 eliminates inverse strict orderings as much as possible so that we arrive at the following reduced profile Π^*:

It is easy to check that a path of binary inversions of adjacent alternatives exists. Such a path can neither be found for the profile

$$
\begin{array}{ccc}
x & y & z \\
y & z & x \\
z & x & y
\end{array}
$$

which, of course, exhibits a Latin Square, nor for the profile

$$
\begin{array}{ccc}
x & y & z \\
y & z & x
\end{array}
$$

which satisfies both value restriction and limited agreement. We are now in a position to define what we call the binary inversion property.

Definition. The reduced equivalent strict preference profile of a given society is said to satisfy the binary inversion property (*BIP*), if (trivially) this profile does not contain more than one type of individual ordering, or if (nontrivially):

$$(N_1 + N_2 + N_3) \cdot (K_1 + K_2 + K_3) > 0.$$

The latter requirement essentially captures the idea of a path composed of binary inversions. This can be easily seen from the three profiles given above in conjunction with the property that $N_j > 0$ implies $K_j = 0$, for all j, as already stated.

When we examine all reduced equivalent strict preference profiles Π^* that are logically possible, we see that

(1) profiles $\Pi^*_{0,0}, \Pi^*_{1,0}, \Pi^*_{1,1}$, and $\Pi^*_{2,1}$ satisfy BIP;

(2) profiles $\Pi^*_{2,0}$ and $\Pi^*_{3,0}$ violate BIP.

We can now state the following result.

Theorem 36 (Gaertner 1988). The method of simple majority decision generates a transitive social relation for a given preference profile Π iff its reduced equivalent strict preference profile Π^* satisfies the binary inversion property for every triple of alternatives.

For original unreduced profiles the condition of extremal restriction has been found to be both necessary and sufficient for collective transitivity under the simple majority rule. What is the logical relationship between condition ER and property BIP? It can be proved (Gaertner 1988) that if the original profile Π fulfils extremal restriction, then the reduced profile Π^* satisfies BIP. As for Saposnik's condition of cyclical balance, the following result holds: An original preference profile satisfies the property of cyclical balance iff the reduced set of preferences either is the empty set or the reduced profile satisfies the condition $(N_1 + N_2 + N_3) \cdot (K_1 + K_2 + K_3) > 0$. Thus, in the latter case, there is a path of binary inversions within the reduced profile.

A sufficient condition for quasi-transitivity (and, of course, for acyclicity) of the social preference relation can easily be stated by modifying the nontrivial requirement in the definition of BIP. If $(N_1 + N_2 + N_3) \cdot (K_1 + K_2 + K_3) = 0$ with any two of the $N_l, l \in \{1,2,3\}$, being strictly positive and the third being zero (any two of the K_l being strictly positive and the third being zero), then simple majority decisions generate a quasi-transitive social relation. The reduced profiles Π^* which fulfil property *BIP* always satisfy both value restriction and limited agreement, once these restrictions are reformulated for Π^*-profiles.

Slutsky (1977) presented sufficient conditions for social transitivity which shed a somewhat different light on Sen's value restriction.[11] Assume that there are only strict individual preferences. Let $m = \min(n_i), i = 1,\ldots,6$, be the smallest number of individuals and $g = \max(n_i)$, $i = 1,\ldots,6$, be the largest number holding one of the six strict orderings. Furthermore, let $h(f)$ be the maximum number (minimum number) of individuals who agree that one alternative in a given triple is strictly best or that one is strictly worst, i.e.

$$h = \max\{N(aP_ib \wedge aP_ic), N(bP_ia \wedge cP_ia),$$
$$\text{for all} \quad (a,b,c) \quad \text{in} \quad (x,y,z)\}$$

and

$$f = \min\{N(aP_ib \wedge aP_ic), N(bP_ia \wedge cP_ia),$$
$$\text{for all} \quad (a,b,c) \quad \text{in} \quad (x,y,z)\}.$$

Then the following result can be stated.

Theorem 37 (Slutsky 1977). For a society consisting of n members with only strict individual orderings, the majority decision will be transitive if either $h > (\frac{1}{2})n - m$ or $f < (\frac{1}{2})n - g$; that is, if there is an alternative which is felt to be strictly best or one which is felt to be strictly worst in the triple by either more than $(\frac{1}{2})n - m$ or less than $(\frac{1}{2})n - g$ individuals.

The conditions in this theorem are, of course, also sufficient for quasi-transitivity of the social preference relation. Weaker conditions, sufficient only for acyclicity over the triple, require that the strict inequalities in the theorem be replaced by weak inequalities (for more details, see Slutsky 1975, 1977). Theorem 37 may lend itself to a reinterpretation of value restriction which is often charac-

---

[11] See also Sen's (1986, p. 1143) own remarks on the role of the median voter within Black's theorem on single-peaked preferences.

terized as expressing a partial agreement or some type of social harmony. It is shown by Slutsky that in cases where a given strict preference profile satisfies condition *VR*, there exists some artificially constructed society where more than half of its members agree that some alternative is strictly best or is strictly worst, thus preventing it being an element in a preference cycle. This fact leads to the interpretation of a weakened type of dominance where a group is not able to dictate the complete social ordering but is able either to impose some alternative as the social choice or to eliminate some alternative from further consideration.

Slutsky did not confine his analysis to societies with only strict individual preferences. Profiles where individuals are indifferent between pairs of alternatives or even reveal intransitive preferences are admissible, too. These profiles, however, are transformed (in a similar way as was done in Gaertner's approach) into equivalent profiles with only strict preferences and the conditions in theorem 37, for example, then apply to these artificially generated preference patterns.

5.2 The design of transitive aggregation procedures

A completely different way to arrive at transitive social relations was suggested by Hosomatsu (1978). This author constructed voting procedures that always yield social preference orderings without imposing any restrictions either on the distribution of individual orderings or on the qualitative structure of preference profiles.

Hosomatsu started out by defining a preference function which assigns real numbers (weights) p_i to individual i's preferences between pairs of alternatives. For example, for any a, b from X,

$$\infty > p_i(a,b) > 0 \quad \text{if} \quad aP_ib,$$
$$-\infty < p_i(a,b) < 0 \quad \text{if} \quad bP_ia,$$
$$p_i(a,b) = 0 \quad \text{if} \quad aI_ib,$$

For elements $x_1, x_2, \ldots, x_k$ from X, let $L(X)$ be the set of k ordered pairs $L(X) = \{(x_1, x_2), (x_2, x_3), \ldots, (x_{k-1}, x_k), (x_k, x_1)\}$. For individual i, a preference vector $\bar{p}_i$ is an ordered k-tuple obtained by applying his preference function $p_i : X \times X \to \mathbb{R}$ to each of the ordered pairs of $L(X)$, i.e. $\bar{p}_i = (p_i(x_1, x_2), p_i(x_2, x_3), \ldots, p_i(x_{k-1}, x_k), p_i(x_k, x_1))$.

A social preference ordering is obtained by finding a social preference vector as the sum of all individual preference vectors $\bar{p}_i$, i.e. $\bar{q} = \Sigma \bar{p}_i$, where the summation is taken over all members i of the society. Given that every individual in society has a transitive preference relation, conditions on the individual preference vectors $\bar{p}_i$ have to be formulated such that the social preference relation is transitive for any possible preference profile. A necessary and sufficient condition for social transitivity turns out to be the so-called 'zero-sum condition'.

For any real vector $\bar{x} = (x_1, x_2, \ldots, x_k)$, let $s(\bar{x})$ be a sum function, defined as the sum over the elements of $\bar{x} : s(\bar{x}) = x_1 + x_2 + \ldots + x_k$. In order to fulfil the zero-sum condition the elements p_i of every individual preference vector $\bar{p}_i$ have to be chosen in such a way that $s(\bar{p}_i) = 0$. We can now formulate

Theorem 38 (Hosomatsu 1978). A necessary and sufficient condition for a voting rule to always generate a transitive social preference relation whenever every individual has transitive preferences is that every individual preference vector $\bar{p}_i$ satisfies the zero-sum condition, namely, $s(\bar{p}_i) = 0$ for all i.

Owing to the zero-sum condition, the weights p_i have to bear a close relationship to the positions of the alternatives within each individual i's preference ordering. Therefore, it is of no surprise that Hosomatsu's suggested voting mechanism does not satisfy Arrow's condition of independence of irrelevant alternatives. Particular examples of aggregation rules in line with Hosomatsu's approach are the well-known Borda rank-order method and Saposnik's (1975a) 'simple contributive rule'.

5.3 Quasi-transitivity of the social preference relation under proper simple games

Let $(N,\mathcal{W},f)$ be a proper simple voting game as defined in subsection 3.5.3 above. Kaneko (1975) has examined this collective choice rule within the context of conditions on the distribution of voters' preferences.[12] For every distinct three alternatives x,y,z we define

$$W(x,y,z) = \{\{i \in N \mid aP_i b\} \mid aPb; a,b \in (x,y,z)\},$$

given an n-tuple of weak orderings $(R_1, \ldots, R_n)$. $W(x,y,z)$ is again interpreted as the collection of winning groups of voters for all pairs $a,b \in (x,y,z)$. Kaneko writes

$$
\begin{aligned}
W(x,y,z) &= \{S\} & \text{if} \quad \#(W(x,y,z)) &= 1 \\
&= \{S,T\} & \text{if} \quad \#(W(x,y,z)) &= 2 \\
&= \{S,T,V\} & \text{if} \quad \#(W(x,y,z)) &= 3.
\end{aligned}
$$

$U(x,y,z)$ is defined in the same way as $U^m(x,y,z)$ was defined in subsection 5.1.1 above (with $W(\ )$ replacing $W^m(\ )$), and we obtain

Theorem 39 (Kaneko 1975). The collective preference relation generated by a proper simple voting game $(N,\mathcal{W},f)$ is quasi-transitive iff for all distinct $x,y,z \in X$, the following condition holds:

$$
\begin{aligned}
&(xP_i y \text{ or } xP_i z & \forall i \in U(x,y,z)) \\
\text{or } &(yP_i x \text{ or } yP_i z & \forall i \in U(x,y,z)) \\
\text{or } &(zP_i x \text{ or } zP_i y & \forall i \in U(x,y,z)) \quad (K^{***}) \\
\text{or } &(yP_i x \text{ or } zP_i x & \forall i \in U(x,y,z)) \\
\text{or } &(xP_i y \text{ or } zP_i y & \forall i \in U(x,y,z)) \\
\text{or } &(xP_i z \text{ or } yP_i z & \forall i \in U(x,y,z)).
\end{aligned}
$$

Note that the domain restrictions are required only for the individuals in $U(x,y,z)$. If the above restrictions had been imposed on the set of all individuals, the upper half and the lower half of condition (K^{***}) would have been the

---

[12] See also Kaneko's analysis at the end of subsection 5.1.1 above and his definition of a necessary condition in n.7 of this chapter.

well-known 'not worst' and 'not best' value restrictions, respectively. We know from theorem 16 in subsection 3.5.3 above that value restriction actually is sufficient for quasi-transitivity of the social preference relation under proper simple voting games.

CHAPTER 6

THE EXISTENCE OF SOCIAL CHOICE
RULES IN n–DIMENSIONAL
CONTINUOUS SPACE

Throughout chapters 2–5, we studied the aggregation problem within the framework of arbitrary finite sets of discrete alternatives. These alternatives could have been political parties or candidates representing these parties, these alternatives could also have stood for well-specified economic and (or) social programmes determining, for example, particular distributions of commodities and particular tax schemes that involve major indivisibilities.

In various economic problems, the possible choices can be envisaged to constitute a set of points in some appropriately defined multi-dimensional choice space, and the individual preferences are represented by quasi-concave, differentiable utility functions defined over this space. The points are n-dimensional vectors which specify, for example, the final consumptions of both private and public goods of all members of the society under consideration. In the present chapter, we shall examine the existence of continuous aggregation rules within such a framework. We also discuss the issue of manipulability in continuous space.

6.1 The standard exclusion conditions in continuous space

Kramer (1973) has shown that for the issue of domain restriction, the transition from finite sets of discrete alternatives to multi-dimensional choice spaces has serious consequences. It is demonstrated that in Euclidean choice space, the standard restriction conditions such as value restriction, extremal restriction and limited agreement are inconsistent with even a modest degree of heterogeneity of individual preferences. More precisely, Kramer proved that if there exists a point x in some open set $S \subset \mathbb{R}^n$ at which the gradient vectors of any three voters i,j,k are linearly independent, the set of preference orderings representable by continuous and differentiable ordinal utility functions does not satisfy any of the proposed exclusion conditions over S.

Consider, for example, the following two-dimensional situation which is taken from Kramer (1973) (figure 6.1). At a point x in $\mathbb{R}^2$, the indifference curves of three individuals 1, 2 and 3 cross in the manner indicated. As can be seen, the marginal rates of substitution of the three voters differ considerably at x. Obviously, the monotonicity property which is a common assumption in the private goods context does not hold in this situation. For the three neighbouring points y,z,w, one observes wP_1yP_1z, zP_2wP_2y and yP_3zP_3w. These orderings form a Latin Square, so none of the standard exclusion conditions is satisfied.

If the condition of linear independence in Kramer's result is somewhat weakened, not all standard exclusion conditions, but only a strict subset of them will be violated. One could argue against the situation in figure 6.1 by saying that a case was chosen where the preferences of the three individuals are very heterogeneous indeed.

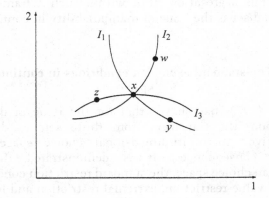

Figure 6.1

However, it can be shown that even if the heterogeneity of tastes is quite mild and the monotonicity property of individuals' preferences fulfilled, standard restriction conditions will be violated.

In figure 6.2, the choice space is again $\mathbb{R}^2$. Let us assume that there exists a point y in $\mathbb{R}^2$ at which the marginal rates of substitution of three voters 1, 2 and 3 differ, but only slightly when compared to figure 6.1. I_1, I_1' and I_1'' are indifference contours of person 1, I_2 and I_2', and I_3, I_3' are indifference curves for persons 2 and 3. I_1', I_2 and I_3' cross at y as depicted. We now introduce alternatives x and z in the neighbourhood of y. For individual 1, the preference ordering is xP_1yP_1z, for individual 2, the ordering is yI_2zP_2x, for person 3, we have zP_3xI_3y (see again our example after theorem 5 in subsection 3.1.1.2).

Clearly, this set of individual orderings in two dimensions violates all of the standard restriction conditions (ER, LA and VR), though the heterogeneity of tastes is quite modest and the monotonicity property is satisfied with respect to all individuals' preferences.

6.2 Impossibility results for continuous choice rules

Most of the existing work in social choice is combinatorial in nature. We now study the problem of aggregation of

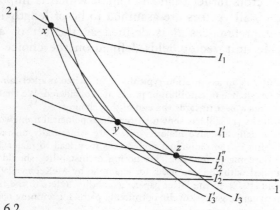

Figure 6.2

individual preferences within a topological framework. In contrast to the standard Arrovian approach, continuity of the social aggregation rule will be required. Chichilnisky (1982a, p. 346, 1997a, p. 193) gives a defence of this assumption. It allows an approximation of social preferences on the basis of a sample of individual orderings and makes mistakes in identifying preferences less crucial. Furthermore continuity is a form of stability of society's choices with respect to small changes in individuals' preferences.[1] In the discrete case, the simple majority rule is unstable in this sense, for even in very large societies a single individual when becoming a pivotal voter can bring about a significant change in the outcome of an election by simply inverting his or her own ordering of alternatives.[2]

We consider a choice space X which is contained in the positive orthant of the n-dimensional Euclidean space $\mathbb{R}^n_+$. Let X be a cube in $\mathbb{R}^n_+$. Each individual preference p_i is a C^1 vector field over the space of alternatives, which is locally integrable. This means that to each alternative x in X, one attaches a vector $p_i(x)$ in a continuously differentiable fashion which indicates the direction of the largest increase of utility. This direction is that of the normal to the tangent plane of the indifference surface through x. Since ordinal preferences are considered it is the direction of the vectors rather than the length which is important. Therefore, all vectors are assumed to be of length 1. The space of preferences P is defined as the set of all C^1 integrable unit vector fields defined on the choice space

---

[1] Continuity is an assumption typically made when market allocations and the existence of equilibrium prices are considered. We shall come back to this aspect towards the end of this chapter.

[2] Chichilnisky (1982b) has shown within the topological framework that what she calls 'decisive majority rules' are structurally unstable, i.e. small shifts in the individual preferences may lead to major changes in the outcome preference. This notion of instability should not be confounded with the one used, for example, by McKelvey (1979) and Schofield (1978). In the latter paper, 'instability' refers to the fact that within dynamic games, cyclic optimizing paths for winning coalitions exist under certain conditions.

X. There are k individuals in society. A social aggregation rule for individual preferences is a function that assigns to each k-tuple of individual preferences (each preference profile) a social preference in P. If Φ stands for a social aggregation rule, we have

$$\Phi : \underbrace{P \times \ldots \times P}_{k\text{-times}} \to P.$$

According to Chichilnisky (1980, 1982a), the rule Φ is required to satisfy the following three properties. First of all, the social preference has to define at each choice a most desirable direction in a continuous manner. The continuity of Φ is defined in terms of convergence in the space of preferences which implies that proximity of preferences in P is equivalent to the proximity of their indifference surfaces. Secondly, the choice rule Φ is assumed to satisfy the condition of anonymity, i.e. $\Phi(p_1,p_2,\ldots,p_k) = \Phi(p_{r(1)},p_{r(2)},\ldots,p_{r(k)})$, where $r(1)$, $r(2)$, $\ldots$, $r(k)$ denotes any permutation of the set of integers $\{1,2,\ldots,k\}$. Thirdly, the choice rule Φ is required to respect unanimity, i.e. $\Phi(p,p,\ldots,p) = p$ for all $p \in P$.

It should be mentioned that respect for unanimity is a condition which is weaker than the Pareto condition since it makes a requirement only in the case where all preferences within a profile are the same. The condition of anonymity is stronger than Arrow's nondictatorship condition (Arrow 1963), because it requires equal treatment of the individuals' preferences, while Arrow's condition only forbids an extreme unevenness of treatment. The following impossibility result can now be stated.

Theorem 40 (Chichilnisky 1980, 1982a, 1983). Any continuous social aggregation rule for smooth individual preferences cannot simultaneously satisfy the conditions of anonymity and respect of unanimity.[3]

---

[3] The impossibility changes into a possibility when the requirement no longer is that a complete social ordering exist on the choice space X but that there always be some optimal social choice $x \in X$ (Chichilnisky 1993).

Though the main theme of this monograph is the discussion of domain conditions and not the presentation of impossibility results, we nevertheless wish to give a geometrical argument underlying the theorem which is also due to Chichilnisky (1982a). Let the choice space X be two-dimensional, a unit cube denoted I^2. Furthermore, let the space of preferences consist of linear preferences only. This space is denoted by Q. Now let 0 be the centre of X. Then each preference Q can be uniquely identified by a point on the circle S^1 (see figure 6.3). Let us further assume that there are only two individuals. For this special case, the theorem states that there exists no continuous map ψ assigning to each pair (p_1, p_2) in S^1 a third point p in S^1 (the social preference), such that

$$\psi(p_1, p_2) = \psi(p_2, p_1), \quad \text{and}$$
$$\psi(p_1, p_2) = p_1 = p_2, \quad \text{if} \quad p_1 = p_2 \quad \text{(unanimity)}.$$

Chichilnisky illustrates her impossibility result by means of an aggregation rule which is some kind of an averaging rule. Let p_1 and p_2 be two vectors in S^1 and let $\psi(p_1, p_2)$ be the unit vector in a direction that is determined by half the angular distance between p_1 and p_2 in the clockwise direction. Now let p_1 rotate clockwise around the unit circle S^1. Then as $p_1 \to p_2, \psi(p_1, p_2)$ must converge to p_3. On the other hand, owing to unanimity, $\psi(p_1, p_2)$ must also converge to p_2, as p_1 converges to p_2. Thus, this anonymous choice rule suggests a clash between continuity and unanimity.

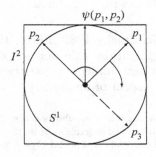

Figure 6.3

The negative result in theorem 40 can be extended to preferences that allow for satiation. Let R denote the space of individual and social preferences which also contains preferences whose gradients may vanish in interior points of the choice space X. A restriction which is imposed on preferences in R is that for each $p \in R$ the set of choices in X, where the gradient $p(x)$ for x in X vanishes, is either a set of measure zero in X or the whole of X. R is endowed with the topology of pointwise convergence of gradients outside of the set of choices where these gradients vanish. For the present result, the unanimity condition has to be replaced by a Pareto condition: If x is preferred (or indifferent) to y for all individuals k and $\Phi(p_1, \ldots, p_k) = p$, then x is socially preferred (or indifferent) to y according to p. The following result holds.

Theorem 41 (Chichilnisky 1982a). There is no continuous social choice rule $\Phi : R \times \ldots \times R \to R$ that is anonymous and satisfies the Pareto condition.

We now wish to examine the issue of manipulability that we have already discussed in earlier chapters. We consider what Chichilnisky (1993) calls an aggregation game, with k players each announcing a preference that is chosen strategically. It may or may not be the true preference of the agent. Only the individuals themselves know their true preferences. Each player i has a true or honest preference p_i and the strategy set of each agent consists of all preferences in Q, the space of linear preferences. With each player announcing a preference, be it the true preference p_i or a strategically chosen preference p_i', a profile of preferences $(p_1, p_2, \ldots, p_k)$ comes about which is the argument of the social aggregation rule Φ. Each agent i evaluates the social outcome $p = \Phi(p_1, \ldots, p_k)$ on the basis of the true preference p_i. Outcomes closer to p_i are preferred to outcomes further away from p_i. A player i is said to be a strategic dictator if for all $k - 1$-tuples of strategies chosen by the others $(p_1, \ldots, p_{i-1}, p_{i+1}, \ldots, p_k)$, there exists a strategy p_i' for agent i such that $\Phi(p_1, \ldots, p_{i-1}, p_i', p_{i+1}, \ldots, p_k) = p_i$. In other words, by playing strategically, agent i can obtain an outcome that is identical to his or her true preference, given any of the $k - 1$-tuples of strategies played by the other agents. Player i is not a dictator in the sense defined earlier, because the announced strategy p_i' may or may not be the true p_i. The following result can be formulated.

Theorem 42 (Chichilnisky 1993). If the social aggregation rule $\Phi : Q \times \ldots \times Q \to Q$ is continuous and respects unanimity, there exists a strategic dictator.

There may be more than one strategic dictator. If this is the case, the aggregation game cannot have a Nash equilibrium when the players have different true preferences.

In Heal (1983), a social aggregation rule Φ is said to be straightforward or nonmanipulable if for each player i, his or her true preference p_i is a dominant strategy. A rule is said to be nontrivially straightforward if it is straightforward and neither dictatorial nor constant. Chichilnisky and Heal (1997) show for a class of generalized single-peaked preferences where indifference surfaces are convex ellipsoids with centre at a bliss point, that an aggregation game is straightforward iff the game is 'locally constant or dictatorial'. The authors circumscribe the latter property as 'piecing together' constant rules and dictatorial rules.

6.3 Possibility results for contractible preference spaces

The results in section 6.2 have shown that in general there does not exist a map Φ from the product of the preference space with itself into the preference space that is simultaneously continuous, satisfies anonymity and respects unanimity. We now wish to ask what kind of meaningful restrictions on individual preferences and profiles of individual preferences exist that guarantee the existence of a social choice rule Φ for any finite number of voters.

Let X again be a topological space and let I be the unit interval of the real line. Then X is said to be contractible if there exists a point $x_o \in X$ and a continuous function $F : X \times I \to X$ such that $F(x,0) = x$ and $F(x,1) = x_o$ for all $x \in X$. The introduction of the condition of contractibility into social choice theory is due to Chichilnisky and Heal

(1983). This condition has been applied before in mathematical economics. Debreu (1952) used this property as a sufficient condition for the existence of an equilibrium point in an exchange economy. Roughly speaking, a contractible space is one that has no holes in it and can, therefore, be contracted continuously through itself into one of its points. The unit disk is, for example, contractible since it has no holes. A simple example of a space which is not contractible is the circle in $\mathbb{R}^2$, or any geometrical figure homeomorphic[4] to it (e.g. the boundary of a square or a triangle). The spaces that are being considered in this section are parafinite CW complexes. They can be expressed as a countable union of finite dimensional spaces.[5]

Heal (1983) pointed out the relationship between contractibility and convexity. Any convex space is contractible. This can easily be seen. Take a convex space X and a point $x_o \in X$. By convexity, $\{(1 - t) \cdot x + t \cdot x_o\} \in X$ for any $x \in X$ and any $t \in [0,1]$. If we now set $F(x,t) = (1 - t) \cdot x + t \cdot x_o$, which is a map of $X \times [0,1] \to X$, we obtain $F(x,0) = x$ and $F(x,1) = x_o$ for all $x \in X$, as required in the definition of contractibility. Any space X homeomorphic to a convex space C can be shown to be contractible. The converse, however, is not true. As an example for the latter assertion, Heal mentions the unit disk in $\mathbb{R}^2$ with a line segment attached to its boundary. Consider two topological spaces A and B, $A \subset B$. Then A is a retract of B if there exists a continuous function $f : B \to A$ such that $f(a) = a$ for all $a \in A$. The function f is said to be a retraction. It can be shown that given any contractible finite space A, there exists a convex space B with $A \subset B$ such that A is a retract of B. For spaces which are manifolds, polyhedra or parafinite CW complexes, any contractible space is a retract of a convex space.

---

[4] Two topological spaces A and B are said to be homeomorphic if there exists a function $h : A \to B$ which is continuous, one to one, onto B, and has a continuous inverse. Intuitively speaking, two spaces are homeomorphic if one can be continuously deformed into the other.

[5] For more details on these spaces, see Chichilnisky and Heal (1983, p. 80).

Heal focuses his discussion of the relationship between contractibility and convexity on an aspect that is particularly important for the issue of aggregation. In a space X, take a k-tuple of points $(x_1, \ldots, x_k)$, each of which is in X and assign to them another point y in X which is their aggregate. In mathematical terms, a map f from the k-fold product of X with itself into X has to be constructed, $f : X \times \ldots \times X \to X$. Let f satisfy continuity.

When X is convex, it certainly admits the following continuous aggregation rule:

$$f(x) = \frac{1}{k} \sum_{i=1}^{k} x_i,$$

which is convex addition. For convex spaces, such a type of aggregation is always possible. For the class of topological spaces considered here, the fact that a contractible space is a retract of a convex space makes it possible to assert the same for contractible spaces. Consider $Y \subset X$, with X being convex and Y contractible, and let $r : X \to Y$ be a retraction. We can then define the rule $g : Y \times \ldots \times Y \to Y$ by

$$g(y_1, \ldots, y_k) = r(f(y_1, \ldots, y_k)).$$

Here the function f maps the k-tuple $(y_1, \ldots, y_k)$ into a point in X, and r then pulls this back to Y. Hence one can also aggregate continuously in contractible spaces. As the reader will easily recognize, the continuous aggregation rule $f(x)$ above satisfies the properties of unanimity and anonymity. The mapping $f(x)$ is a particular element from the class of means. This mean obviously fulfils the three conditions Chichilnisky requires to be satisfied by an aggregation rule in continuous space. Horvath (1996) points out that the study of various types of means in mathematics goes back to Kolmogorov. We shall take up this observation again after presenting the main results of this section.

Chichilnisky and Heal (1983) distinguish between restrictions on the types of preferences that can be held by individuals and properties of spaces of profiles (condition on profiles). In both cases, the essential point is that the domain of individual preferences P should be contractible. Consider preferences at a choice y in Y. A preference is then fully determined by the normalized gradient vector $p_i(y)$ giving individual i's preferred direction at y. If there are no restrictions at all on individual preferences, then this normalized gradient vector may take any direction, so the set of possible preferences at the point y is isomorphic to the set of points on the unit sphere centred at y. This is denoted by S^{n-1}, the $(n-1)$-dimensional sphere in $\mathbb{R}^n$ (see S^1 again in figure 6.3). A restriction on individual preferences now takes the form of the specification of a subset of S^{n-1} within which the normalized gradient vector must lie. Let us repeat: With no restrictions, the space of individual preferences at a point is S^{n-1}, and this $(n-1)$-dimensional unit sphere is not contractible, as we already know. If, however, there is a convex cone C of directions, no matter how small, which no individual may have as most preferred directions, the space of preferences becomes $P^c = S^{n-1}\backslash(S^{n-1} \cap C)$, and this space is contractible (see figure 6.4 which illustrates this case for $\mathbb{R}^2$). Within the space of linear preferences, the contractible space P^c is extremely general. The cone C can be arbitrarily small as long as its interior is nonempty. For the case of general smooth preferences a similar statement can be made. If P is the overall space of smooth preferences, define a subspace $\tilde{P}$ of the space P in the following way:

$$\tilde{P} = \{p \in P : p(y) \notin C \quad \text{for all} \quad y \in Y\}.$$

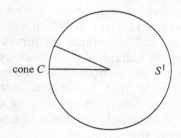

cone C S^1

Figure 6.4

As with P^c above, $\tilde{P}$ is a space of preferences such that all individuals agree that there is one direction of preference which is totally undesirable. In particular, the space of all smooth nondecreasing preferences is contained in $\tilde{P}$, and is contractible. The same statement holds for the space of all smooth, convex and monotone preferences.

There are still weaker restrictions which ensure contractibility. For example, the cone C of excluded directions need not be constant. Consider the space

$$\tilde{P} = \{p \in P : p(y) \notin C_y \quad \text{for all} \quad y \in Y\},$$

where C_y is now a cone of excluded directions at y which varies with y and does so in a smooth way. This space is still contractible. Another example for a contractible preference space is a neat one-dimensional submanifold of the choice space along which all members of the family of C^1 locally integrable preferences are increasing. All foregoing examples for admissible spaces share a common feature: in some way or other, the range of permitted variation in individual preferences is limited.

Coming back to the distinction between restrictions on the type of individuals' preferences and conditions on profiles, in the first case the requirement is that the preferences in the space of preferences are sufficiently similar so that they can be simultaneously continuously deformed to a single preference. In the second case, the requirement is that within any admissible profile there must be sufficient agreement that the preferences in that profile can be continuously deformed into one single preference or a homogeneous profile. What is then required is a sufficiently high level of agreement in any preference profile. Chichilnisky and Heal (1983, p. 75) speak of 'topological unanimity'. This condition limits the types of disagreement among individual preferences, thus determining the variation in preferences which can be accepted. The authors emphasize that topological unanimity is much weaker than unanimity. A set may be quite large and it can still be continuously deformed to a point.

Let us now consider the theorems.

Theorem 43 (Chichilnisky and Heal 1983). Let the space of preferences P be a parafinite CW complex and let k be the number of individuals. Then for all $k \geq 2$ a necessary and sufficient condition for the existence of a social choice rule from the k-fold Cartesian product of P to P which is continuous, anonymous and respects unanimity is that the space of preferences P be contractible.[6]

The next result gives a characterization of the social aggregation rules that can be defined on contractible spaces.

Theorem 44 (Chichilnisky and Heal 1983; Heal 1983). Let the preference space P be contractible. Then any continuous anonymous social choice rule that respects unanimity is equivalent to a rule f constructed as follows. Take a convex space C of which P is a retract, with r the retraction, $r : C \to P$. Then define a convex averaging rule on C, and let f be the composition of this with r.

Equivalence in the above formulation means the following. Two maps are equivalent if they can be linked by a parameterized family of maps $F(x,t)$ which are jointly continuous in x and parameter t, where $x \in X$, some topological space, and $t \in [0,1]$.

For the case that P is convex, we have already indicated that

$$\Phi(p_1, \ldots, p_k) = \frac{1}{k} \sum_{i=1}^{k} p_i,$$

would be an appropriate choice rule according to theorem 44. If P is not convex but contractible, then the composite map

$$\Phi(p_1, \ldots, p_k) = r \circ \left(\frac{1}{k} \sum_{i=1}^{k} p_i \right)$$

defines a continuous anonymous rule that respects unanimity.

---

[6] If the space of preferences is not connected, the theorem requires that every connected component of the space be contractible.

We would like to come back to the remark that means have been analysed in mathematics long before they were studied in social choice theory. According to Horvath (1996),[7] Aumann (1943) analysed a function he called an n-mean. The problem he posed was as follows: Given an abstract space X and a positive integer n, is there a continuous function $M_n : X \times \ldots \times X \to X$ which is anonymous and unanimous (our terminology)? Aumann's result was that if $k \geq 1$, then there is no n-mean on the k-dimensional sphere. We have encountered a similar result above for X being a topological space. Aumann also realized that if there is an n-mean on a topological space X, then there is an n-mean on each connected component of X and there is an n-mean on any retract of X.

Eckmann (1954) stated among other results that contractibility is a necessary and sufficient condition for a connected polyhedron to have an n-mean for each n. Horvath (1996) points out that this result also applies to a wider class of spaces, among them manifolds, absolute neighbourhood retracts and CW complexes, with finitely generated homotopy or homology groups. The sphere is a parafinite CW complex or more simply a finite dimensional polyhedron with finitely generated homology groups. Eckmann, Ganea and Hilton (1962) showed that a polyhedron with finitely generated homology groups and with all the groups trivial but for a finite number of them, cannot have an n-mean, for any given $n \geq 2$, unless it is contractible. If it is contractible, then it has an n-mean for each $n \geq 1$ (see Horvath 1996 for further details).

Let us return to the social choice framework and the issue of manipulability. Clearly, if a game is such that one agent is a dictator or if the outcome of the game is constant, there is no incentive to misrepresent one's preferences. Is there a possibility result beyond these rather trivial cases? In the following, the spaces considered are smooth manifolds X, of dimension at least 5, and with simply connected boundaries.

---

[7] I am grateful to Charles Horvath for allowing me to quote from his unpublished historical review and analysis.

Theorem 45 (Chichilnisky 1983). A continuous nonmanipulable game $g : X \times \ldots \times X \to X$ respecting anonymity exists iff X is contractible.

This result shows a close link between the conditions required for the existence of a social aggregation rule and those needed for the existence of nontrivially straightforward or nonmanipulable games. The necessary and sufficient condition in both cases is contractibility.

6.4 Discrete vs. continuous and the choice of topology

One of the messages which clearly emanate from the analysis in this chapter is that the assumption of continuity is less innocuous than it is often thought. In many contexts, continuity is viewed as a technical assumption, made not for realism but because it simplifies and facilitates the analysis. In microeconomic analysis, for example, the assumption of continuous utility and production functions allows us to use differential calculus instead of applying separation theorems for convex sets. What Chichilnisky and others have shown is that continuity cannot be viewed as merely technical. Theorem 40 demonstrates that under continuity, anonymity and unanimity are mutually inconsistent. Baigent (1997) justly asks whether continuity could perhaps be derived from more basic principles, thus rendering the arguments for requiring this assumption more compelling.

Horvath (2001) has drawn attention to the fact that the existence of social choice rules is not limited to contractible spaces. The author mentions the space of rational numbers with the topology induced by the topology of the real line and the space of irrational numbers with the topology induced by the topology of the real line. Both spaces admit social choice rules. In the first case, take the average of n rational numbers which again is a rational number. In the second case, use the maximum of n irrational numbers which again is an irrational number. While neither of the two spaces is contractible and both are finite dimensional and have

113

nontrivial topologies, they do not appear to be terribly interesting for economic analysis.

In their investigation of the Chichilnisky impossibility results which we have presented in section 6.2, Le Breton and Uriarte (1990a, 1990b) consider a mapping ψ, which for each preference profile $(p_1, p_2, \ldots, p_k)$ of ordinal, nonsatiated linear preferences over the unit cube in $\mathbb{R}^n$ is defined by

$$\psi(p_1, p_2, \ldots, p_k) = \begin{cases} \dfrac{p_1 + \ldots + p_k}{\|p_1 + \ldots + p_k\|}, & \text{if } \displaystyle\sum_{i=1}^{k} p_i \neq 0 \\[2ex] 0 & \text{otherwise.} \end{cases}$$

Note that this mapping contains in its range the null preference $\{0\}$. The topology which the authors select is equivalent to the Kannai (1970) topology when restricted to ordinal, non-satiated linear preferences. For this topology, the above mapping is continuous, anonymous and respects unanimity. Furthermore, in the case of an extreme conflict with strictly opposed preferences p and $-p$, the above mapping generates complete indifference among all alternatives, the null preference $\{0\}$, as the social outcome. For Le Breton and Uriarte, this result seems natural in the case of extreme disagreement. On the other hand, Chichilnisky's choice of topology would make it impossible to select $\{0\}$ as the outcome in such a situation. Her continuity requirement does not allow total indifference among all choices.[8] Le Breton and Uriarte argue that a social choice rule should solve extreme conflicts in a continuous way. 'Therefore, the choice of a particular topology can be an indirect way of excluding the possibility of solving extreme conflicts and, in turn, of producing an impossibility result' (Le Breton and Uriarte 1990a, p. 134; 1990b, p. 147).

One should not overlook, however, that Chichilnisky's framework admits preferences with vanishing gradients in

---

[8] It may help to have another look at the illustration in figure 6.3 in section 6.2, where p_2 and p_3 are strictly opposed. For the continuity issue involved, see also Chichilnisky (1982a).

the interior of the choice space (see theorem 41 above). What is not allowed within her topology are 'larger areas' of social indifference, and we find it legitimate to ask whether a social choice mechanism that, under certain conditions, ends up with an equivalence among all choice alternatives, has really solved the aggregation problem. It is perhaps worth mentioning here that in the discrete framework, the transitive closure method, based on simple majority counting, leads to complete social indifference among all alternatives in the case of a Latin Square preference profile. Apart from violating the Pareto principle in many cases, this aggregation procedure often proves unable to screen among the alternatives. Can it then be considered to yield acceptable solutions? On the other hand, one has to admit that a Condorcet triple or Latin Square profile of individual orderings is different from a situation where two individuals simply have strictly opposite preferences, as discussed above. Le Breton and Uriarte's argument for complete indifference sounds persuasive in this case.

In their own analysis which Le Breton and Uriarte call the 'global approach', the two authors choose the topology of closed convergence, a topology which has been extensively used in equilibrium theory (see, e.g., Hildenbrand 1974). The authors show (1990a) that the space of strictly convex preferences defined on a locally compact set and endowed with the closed convergence topology admits continuous and anonymous aggregation rules that satisfy unanimity. Another possibility result for the case that the space of preferences is endowed with the topology of closed convergence was established by Allen (1996). She shows that for preferences which are complete preorders and satisfy continuity and monotonicity, a continuous aggregation rule exists that satisfies unanimity and anonymity. Allen mentions that her social aggregation procedure does not work for the case of convex or strictly convex preferences, since under the utility representation mapping that is used, the set of utilities derived from (strictly) convex preference relations need not be convex. Hence, the averages of the utility representations may correspond to preference orderings that fail to be convex.

Chichilnisky (1991) has proved that the space of strictly convex preferences on a compact set with the closed convergence topology is contractible. Le Breton and Uriarte's construction of an aggregation rule does not generalize to the whole space of continuous preferences (which is not contractible) but, of course, they have never made such a claim. Allen's assumption of monotone preferences is a standard requirement in equilibrium analysis. Within social choice theory it is, however, quite contentious. Social alternatives are different from private ones. Imagine, for example, a social decision over the composition of a federal budget where one of the various components concerns welfare expenditure, another one defence expenditure. One individual's preference may be monotone in welfare with a smaller defence budget, however, always being preferred to a larger one. Another person may have just the opposite preference. If all individuals' preferences satisfy the monotonicity property, there clearly exists some angle or cone of preference directions that nobody wants to claim. If all the other directions are permitted, we have a situation as in figure 6.4 above. The space of preferences is contractible.[9]

Is there a justification for choosing a particular topology in the social choice framework? Le Breton and Uriarte remark that 'the closed convergence topology has some appeal in mathematical economics' (1990a, p. 136), and they continue saying that 'what we are doing here is just following the tradition started in general competitive analysis' (1990a, p. 136). We feel that this is not an entirely convincing answer to the problem. Baigent and Huang (1990) observe that in general equilibrium theory the intuition is that agents whose choices are similar, from all possible budget sets, must have similar preferences. This means that the concept of closeness of preferences derives from a concept of closeness of the manifestations of preferences. But does this argument have a deeper relevance in social choice theory where

---

[9] See also Chichilnisky (1982a, 1996).

social alternatives are being ranked, alternatives that cannot be viewed as choices from budget sets, as in market analysis?

On the other hand, Baigent and Huang contend that the smooth topology chosen by Chichilnisky also lacks a firm justification for its use in social choice theory. For which issue in collective choice theory, so they ask, does one require smoothness of preferences? Baigent and Huang then argue that the concept of closeness of preferences should be dealt with within the finite framework, and they refer to Kemeny and Snell's (1962) metric on preferences. In the finite framework, the concept of continuity is replaced by the requirement that a social aggregation rule preserve proximity. Baigent (1987) has shown that both for social welfare functions and for social choice functions there exists an incompatibility among the properties of anonymity, unanimity and proximity preservation in the 'finite world', a result that can be viewed as an analogue of Chichilnisky's impossibility result.

The issue of which topology to choose in the case where the choice space has a richer structure than a finite one is truly an important and interesting one. Equally important, perhaps more important for social choice theory, is the question whether the finite framework or the topological framework is the more appropriate one to work in. Traditional welfare economics (see, e.g., Graaff 1967 or Boadway and Bruce 1984) abounds with the use and analysis of smooth indifference curves.[10] The (infinitely many) points which make up a particular indifference surface represent different bundles that vary continuously in the composition of their components.[11] In a collective decision on the composition of a federal budget, the individual voter who draws up his or her indifference

---

[10] Remember that this branch of economics was developed out of microeconomics where indifference curves and isoquants have always been a basic tool of analysis.

[11] For a philosopher's view on indifference curves and trade-offs, see Steiner (1994, chap. 5c).

curve is envisioned as viewing a certain amount of public services, combined with a certain quantity of public investment and a particular scheme of direct and indirect taxation, each component representing some real number, as equivalent to many other vectors (strictly speaking, to an infinite number of vectors) having different compositions of their components. The marginal rate of substitution is typically changing along the indifference surface and is varying among the members of society. In this and several other cases, it makes sense indeed to use some kind of an averaging rule, as has been presented in section 6.3, in order to generate the 'socially preferred vector' (the socially best federal budget).

On the other hand, very often, so it seems, the members of society are confronted with a finite number of clearly specified options which represent different economic and (or) social programmes, and the individuals are asked to work out their own ranking of these discrete alternatives. This task is being performed within a finite framework with no trace whatsoever of smooth indifference curves. There definitely are lots of discrete choice alternatives and the social outcome over these alternatives does not (cannot by its very nature) change in infinitesimally small amounts. As typical social choice examples, we have already referred to party programmes, political candidates, investment projects. But there are many more as, for example, the creation of new institutions such as the European Central Bank (ECB), the introduction of a new European currency, a possible separation of the province of Québec from the rest of Canada or, during the Cold War era, the construction of so and so many missile sites and/or the deployment of so and so many nuclear warheads. Of course, one could, for example, imagine decomposing the ECB into its (future) functionings or consequences and then focus on the rate of inflation of the Euro, the value of the latter against the dollar and the yen, and the rate of unemployment in the European member countries, but this view seems to be a bit contrived. 'Common' people hardly think in terms of vectors of real numbers in this context. Moreover, neither

118

economists nor politicians would be able to give reliable numbers in the first place. Interestingly enough, in his defence of the topological approach to social choice, Heal (1997, p. 156) mentions in relation to the securities business many collective decisions that determine 'the laws which regulate the organization and conduct of the industry'. But can laws be varied continuously?

Our argument above was that there are many discrete alternatives which are the object of social choice. But there is another aspect which cannot be (completely) separated from the foregoing. And we now wish to refer again to Chichilnisky's argument that continuity is a form of stability of society's choices with respect to small changes in individuals' preferences (see section 6.2 above). In the arena of politics, Weingast (1995) observed that '*policy outcomes are not a smooth function of public opinion*' (emphasis in the original). And he continued that 'explaining a major policy change ... requires not only an examination of public opinion but how public opinion is aggregated via the relevant institutions and, in particular, how it affects the identity and preferences of those who control the agenda' (1995, p. 17). Admittedly, Weingast's argument involves the aspect of implementation and this is different from the aspect of evaluation (in terms of a social welfare function), but both aspects are not totally disjoint. Chichilnisky herself (1997c) emphasizes, when she introduces her framework, the institutional requirements that are needed to 'organize effectively a diverse society' (p. 122).

Another aspect in the continuity debate is that political elections can produce narrow majorities which then shape politics over a longer period. The point is not so much that an election is won just by one vote (this is highly unlikely in a larger election, though electoral systems are known where the returning officer had a casting vote if ever there was a tie) but that the distribution of seats in the representative body is such that the winning party may have a majority of just one seat. Such narrow majorities can also be brought about by coalition formation, a procedure which is quite common within the political landscape of continental Europe.[12] Adenauer, the first chancellor of the Federal Republic of Germany, was elected by the narrow margin of one vote (his own vote, people say).[13] During his chancellorship, the first after the collapse of Hitler's Germany, quite a few far-reaching decisions were taken for West Germany. In retrospect, perhaps, the most important decision of Adenauer's government was to embed the western part of Germany in the western hemisphere (and alliance).

The arguments in this section are meant to show that there is room for more than one framework and for more than one technique. Coming back to the topological approach, Chichilnisky (1991) gives two more reasons why the continuous framework is needed. 'One is to obtain new and useful results which are not obtainable, not even understandable, otherwise' (1991, p. 315), and she mentions the contractibility property as a necessary and sufficient domain condition to avoid impossibility results in continuous spaces. Note that such a general necessary and sufficient condition is not available within the finite

[12] One example for this are the elections in Hesse on 7 February 1999 where the Christian Democrats together with the Free Democrats managed to topple the incumbent, a coalition between the Social Democrats and the Green Party, with 56 seats in Parliament for the new coalition against 54 seats for the old. Counting votes during the election night was a nail-biting affair, since for several hours it was not clear whether the Free Democrats would be able to meet the 5 per cent clause. With precisely 3,197 votes less for the Free Democrats (out of 2,843,982 votes cast), not only would the party have been expelled from Parliament, but the incumbent would have been able to retain a *comfortable* majority, no continuity at all.

[13] On 15 September 1949 Adenauer received 202 out of 402 votes in the Deutscher Bundestag. According to the records, Adenauer did not abstain.

A pivotal vote on a discrete alternative can, of course, be cast within a 'much more mundane' setting. *The New York Times* reported in its issue of 1 March 1991 that a woman cast the pivotal vote to give New York City's high schools the nation's first full condom distribution programme. Another very narrow decision came about when the issue was where to hold the 2006 World Cup tournament.

framework,[14] but note also that her argument is acceptable only to those who are convinced that one should go beyond the combinatorial techniques of finite social choice.

Chichilnisky's second argument for needing calculus and topology 'is the integration of Social Choice into the general body of Economic Theory' (1991, p. 316). At first sight, this reasoning does not appear entirely convincing. Why shouldn't it be the case that within economics different areas use different techniques? The theory of the business cycle, for example, uses linear and nonlinear differential and difference equations while equilibrium theory applies set theory and topological methods. The underlying issues may also require different analytical techniques. Arrow (1951, 1963) began his famous monograph by saying that 'in a capitalist democracy there are essentially two methods by which social choices can be made: voting ... and the market mechanism ... The methods of voting and the market ... are methods of amalgamating the tastes of many individuals in the making of social choices.' The reader knows very well that Arrow's book is almost entirely talking about social decision-making and not about the role and the rule of the price mechanism.

In a series of papers Chichilnisky (1994, 1995, 1997a, 1997c), however, made an attempt to bridge social choice and equilibrium theory by using topological methods. The key concept for this link is the notion of social diversity and a limitation on this, called limited arbitrage. The author asserts that limited arbitrage is necessary and sufficient for the existence of a competitive equilibrium. She then links limited arbitrage with contractibility of the space of preferences the role of which for the existence of a continuous social choice rule we discussed in section 6.3. She finally claims that limited arbitrage eliminates Condorcet

---

[14] Of course, at various instances in this monograph, the reader was introduced to necessary and sufficient conditions for the existence of social choice rules. In the discrete framework, these conditions were always stated with reference to a particular aggregation rule (such as simple majority rule, special majority rules, simple voting games, etc.).

cycles on choices of large utility values and thus contributes to a resolution of Arrow's impossibility result.

Chichilnisky defines 'arbitrage' as an opportunity for an agent to increase his or her utility level costlessly beyond the level associated with any given vector in his or her consumption set. Limited arbitrage rules out such an arbitrage. More technically, limited arbitrage as the nonempty intersection of the individual traders' market cones means that there exists a price vector at which the traders can afford only limited increases in utility from their initial endowments. The market cone of a trader is the cone of prices assigning strictly positive value to all directions of net trades leading to eventually increasing utility. The definition of a trader's market cone rests on the concept of a global cone corresponding to an agent's utility function. Chichilnisky (1997a, p. 166) defines the global cone of an agent as the cone of net trades along which utility increases without bound.

The years since 1994 have witnessed a lively and, admittedly, rather controversial discussion around Chichilnisky's claim that the condition of limited arbitrage is necessary and sufficient for the existence of an economic equilibrium. It is impossible to mention, let alone discuss all the issues that are involved in this intricate altercation.[15] Apparently the dispute requires that several distinctions be made. Is the space to be considered $\mathbb{R}^n_+$ or $\mathbb{R}^n$, the latter admitting unbounded short sales? Are half-lines in indifference surfaces allowed or are they excluded? Furthermore, is the concept of global cone used in the claim properly defined? The interested reader will have to find his or her own way through a myriad of

.[15] See, among other contributions, Page and Wooders (1994); Chichilnisky (1997b); Monteiro, Page and Wooders (1997, 1999). Monteiro, Page and Wooders (1997), for example, argue that the condition of limited arbitrage as defined by Chichilnisky has not been shown to be sufficient for existence of an equilibrium. The three authors claim that Chichilnisky's condition is necessary only for existence. This is disputed by Chichilnisky (1997b). Unfortunately, various typographical errors, for example in figure 4B on p. 88 of Chichilnisky (1995), complicate the debate.

examples and counter-examples in order to understand the arguments and counter-arguments given on either side.

As a final point in this section, we would like to add a few words to Chichilnisky's claim that limited arbitrage is a necessary and sufficient condition 'for a resolution of Arrow's paradox on choices of large utility value' (1997a, theorem 28). This statement is surprising indeed since for several reasons the limited arbitrage condition and a condition for resolving Arrow's problem seem to belong to 'two different worlds'. Baryshnikov (1997, p. 200) writes that Chichilnisky 'has shown that, for choices involving large utility values, her formulation and Arrow's are equivalent'.[16] How can this be?

The first thing to say is that Arrow's axiom system and Chichilnisky's axiomatic set-up, discussed in section 6.2, are logically independent.[17] We have already pointed out that respect of unanimity is a condition weaker than the Pareto requirement. Anonymity is stronger than Arrow's nondictatorship condition. Continuity and Arrow's independence requirement are logically unrelated.

The next point refers to Chichilnisky's proposition (1997a, p. 177) that an economy, defined on $\mathbb{R}^n_+$ or $\mathbb{R}^n$ with individual initial endowments from $\mathbb{R}^n_+$ and individual continuous and convex preferences, has limited arbitrage iff for some $k > 0$, the traders' preferences have no Condorcet cycles of size larger than k.[18] This proposition is the building block in the alleged connection between limited arbitrage and Arrow's result. Two observations seem to be in order here. First, Arrow never considered choices of small and/or large utility value in the proof of his impossibility theorem; 'small' and 'large' do

---

[16] Baryshnikov (1993) himself developed a topological approach which allowed him to re-prove Arrow's impossibility result. The author uses the notion of a simplicial complex.

[17] As a matter of fact, Chichilnisky (1997a, p. 193) made the same observation.

[18] A 'cycle of size larger than k' means that three feasible allocations that form a Condorcet cycle give to each agent involved a utility level of at least size k.

not make sense in an ordinal framework where arbitrary strictly monotonic transformations are permissible.[19] Staying within Chichilnisky's argumentation for a moment, one could then, of course, ask how the resolution argument would fare for choices of smaller utility value. Secondly, the Condorcet cycle is not an indispensable component within Arrow's construction of his proof. The inconsistency can already be shown for three alternatives and two individuals. In other words, the full Condorcet cycle is not needed.

The foregoing criticism is by no means meant to belittle Chichilnisky's attempt to establish a relationship between market allocations through the price mechanism and social allocations via an aggregation rule, the two methods Arrow was speaking of. On the contrary, this undertaking of unification is an interesting and truly challenging one. However, it seems to us that there is still some need for further clarification.

---

[19] On the other hand, the aspect of large utility values seems indispensable in Chichilnisky's argument, since limited arbitrage, according to the author, bounds the traders' utility gains.

CHAPTER 7

CONCLUDING REMARKS

After the collapse of socially planned economies, the market is the predominant mechanism. But even in most of the market-oriented economies, many dimensions of resource allocation, as Heal (1997, p. 156) notes, 'are within the domain of political decision-making, and are therefore determined by social choices'. Heal mentions defence, education, the health care sector and investments in infrastructure. These sectors, taken together, account for a large portion of GNP in most industrialized countries. So social choices and public decision-making are an integral part of modern industrial economies and their functionings.

This monograph has been about domain restrictions in social choice theory. Do such restrictions actually exist or are they nothing else but the outgrowth of the scientist's imagination or phantasy? This question may sound purely rhetorical after many pages full of logical analysis around the issue of whether conditions on individual preferences exist that guarantee the existence of a social welfare function or a social decision rule or a continuous aggregation function.

In the section on the likelihood of cyclical majorities we cited Sen (1970, p. 164) who remarked that 'the equiprobability assumption (of individual orderings) *is* a very special one, and seems to involve a denial of society, in a significant sense' (emphasis in the original). And he continued that owing to people's values and group interests there would be 'a fair amount of link-up' among individuals' preferences. This seems to be a widespread opinion among those who in their writings either discussed domain conditions or actively contributed to this area. Luce and Raiffa (1957) formulated very carefully that 'if

125

we do not demand too much versatility of a social choice function' (p. 354), there are ways of side-stepping Arrow's impossibility theorem. The authors thought of reasonable restrictions on preference profiles and defined 'reasonable in the sense that they do not rule out all practical, non-trivial cases' (p. 353). They added that 'for example, we might assume that there is some underlying structure to preferences which prohibits extreme divergences of opinion' (p. 341). Pattanaik (1971) raised the following question: 'why should we require an unrestricted domain? Assume that some set of individual orderings do not belong to the domain of the social welfare function. But if we know that these sets of individual orderings are unlikely to be found in real life then we need not be very much disturbed by the fact that they do not belong to the domain of the SWF' (p. 49). Batra and Pattanaik (1972b) reiterated this statement by saying that if in any society there are some similarities of preferences, 'it will be enough if the group decision rule can cope with only those configurations that are likely to arise in real life' (p. 3).

Marglin (1995) read Arrow's impossibility result in the sense that 'every (nondictatorial) society must have a means of forming and instilling mutually consistent individual preferences as the condition of its survival without a dictator', and he went on to say that 'in practice, the requisite homogenization of preferences is accomplished by culture. Indeed, we might say that it is the function of culture to allow society to operate without the need for dictatorship'.[1]

Already 'in the early days' after Arrow's impossibility result, Graaff (1962) argued that the possibility of intransitivity of the social preference relation might be less important than it appears from the theoretical analysis.

---

[1] The logic behind this argumentation and, for example, Luce and Raiffa's statements referred to earlier is quite obvious: in order to avoid Arrow's impossibility it does not suffice to delete logically possible orderings (admissible under the condition of unrestricted domain) in an arbitrary fashion. The deletion has to be done with reason. Note on the other hand that in the proof of his impossibility result, Arrow did not need the full spectrum of logically possible orderings.

'That is because, if a society is to cohere at all, let alone function as a political unit, its members must in some measure share a common ethic.' In our introduction to this monograph we quoted Sen (1970, p. 165) arguing that 'individual preferences are determined not by turning a roulette wheel over all possible alternatives, but by certain specific social, economic, political, and cultural forces. This may easily produce some patterns in the set of individual preferences.'[2] In a statement in the *New Palgrave* (1987, p. 385) Sen is more careful and offers some differentiation: 'when the number of alternatives happens to be small, and when there is complex balancing of conflicting considerations, as in many political contexts (elections, committee decisions over rival proposals, etc.), there might possibly be some room for optimism. If cycles or other types of intransitivities turn out to be rather rare in these cases, then the approach of domain restriction may well offer some help.' However, he then continues 'in contrast, in welfare-economic problems, that hope is very limited'. To substantiate the latter assertion, Sen refers to the division-of-a-cake-problem. Let us assume that there are three individuals who have monotonic preferences with respect to their own share only. Suppose the three alternative divisions for this three-person society are $a = (\frac{1}{3}, \frac{1}{3}, \frac{1}{3})$, $b = (\frac{3}{4}, 0, \frac{1}{4})$, and $c = (\frac{2}{5}, \frac{2}{5}, \frac{1}{5})$. Let the three preference orderings be bP_1cP_1a, cP_2aP_2b, and aP_3bP_3c. We have a Latin Square. Thus, simple majority rule generates cyclical social preferences. There is nothing pathological about the individuals' orderings so that the majority cycle occurs quite naturally. However, for a slightly different set of alternatives, one could also launch a counter-argument. Change alternative b into $b' = (\frac{1}{2}, 0, \frac{1}{2})$ and assume again that the persons are monotonic in their own share of the cake. This time person 3 will have bP_3aP_3c, the profile now satis-

---

[2] In their empirical analysis mentioned before, Feld and Grofman (1987) defined an individual's *ideological* (emphasis added) preference ordering, given a particular unidimensional continuum, as one which is based on an ideal point, having a peak there and declining in both directions from that peak.

fies the property of single-cavedness so that the method of majority decision generates a transitive social relation. For the modified set of alternatives, the assumption of monotonic preferences introduces a natural restriction which 'saves the day'. Some social choice theorists have argued that social decisions over public goods are the ones that create problems, since *a priori* restrictions of individual preferences do not make much sense in these cases. In the quotation given above, Luce and Raiffa suspected that extreme divergences of opinion might be a problem, but if 'extreme divergences' are interpreted in the sense of strictly opposing ('antagonistic') preferences, we know from chapter 3 that there is no problem at all. The fact is, however, and one can easily see this in the case of the Condorcet paradox, that one single 'wrong' ordering added to an 'orderly' preference profile can bring about 'disorder'. Consider one thousand voters having the preference *aPbPcPd*, another one thousand voters stating *bPcPdPa*, yielding a single-peaked profile and add one individual with the ordering *dPaPbPc*. A 'disorderly' preference cycle is the immediate consequence. Or take an example from Feld and Grofman (1987), where eight voters have *aPbPc*, five state *bPcPa* and four have *cPbPa*. Now allow one among the last four voters to change from *cPbPa* to *cPaPb*. Single-peakedness is no longer given and a majority cycle arises.

Are we attaching too much importance to the occurrence of cycles? At this point, we wish to come back to the aspect of implementation that was already briefly mentioned towards the end of chapter 6. Tullock (2000) argued that the reason why there are no majority cycles in practice is that the final vote very often 'is a "yes" or "no" on a single proposal, and that proposal is a result of a long process of shaping and changes' (p. 4).[3] Shaping and

---

[3] This statement is somewhat in contrast to findings by Riker (1958) and others, reported in Gehrlein (1983). Riker examined congressional voting results when two or more amendments were considered with the original bill. Riker estimated that majority voting cycles occurred in more than 10 per cent of these cases.

changes are the outcome of negotiations carried on in private long before bills get to the floor. Shepsle and Weingast (1982) criticized the instability results of pure majority rule, to which we briefly referred in n.2 of chapter 6, by not taking account of 'a complex series of institutional arrangements underpinning the operation of majority rule legislatures' (p. 367). The theoretical result that the majority rule may 'wander around' in the space of alternatives no longer holds if agenda formation is considered. Real-world legislatures 'typically institute complex agenda formation games with a fixed sequence of access to the agenda and constraints upon the content of the agenda' (p. 368). Leininger (1993) showed that the decision of the Deutscher Bundestag to move parliament and government from Bonn to Berlin was profoundly influenced by the choice of agenda. A different procedure would have generated a different outcome. A majority vote on all relevant alternatives (actually three) simultaneously was not part of the agenda. Such a vote would have been indecisive according to the reconstructed preferences of the representatives in parliament.

The monograph has discussed different types of domain restrictions. We started out by analysing various qualitative restrictions on preference profiles. Single-peaked preferences as well as antagonistic and dichotomous preferences (the latter as subcases of the requirement of extremal restriction) are relatively easy to interpret. In our view, one of these restrictions – single-peakedness, stands out in particular. Not only did it prove to be a central restriction under majority voting, it also played an essential role in the context of strategy-proof voting rules.[4] Of course, we do not have any reason to believe that in a particular voting situation, all members of a committee will show single-peaked or value restricted preferences, though single-peakedness or single-cavedness may be 'quite natural' properties in a variety of real-world

---

[4] Single-peakedness has also been found to be important in problems of fair division (see Thomson 1994, 1998 and Klaus 1998, among others).

contexts. In a situation where everybody in a committee knows precisely the preference ordering of everybody else, it may be the case that some committee member will alter his or her preferences in order to prevent a deadlock owing to a majority cycle (see again n.12 in the introduction) but the reader may, perhaps, find this view a bit too idealistic.

We have also considered quantitative or number-specific requirements on the distribution of voters over different preference orderings, and we saw that some of those requirements are logically related to the qualitative restrictions. While the latter conditions are restrictions on combinations of individual orderings, Kalai and Muller's domain condition for the existence of a non-dictatorial n-person social welfare function and various other requirements are restrictions on permissible preferences for individuals. Contractibility as a condition on the topological space of preferences again is of a different nature – though basically, it is a condition requiring limited variability of individual preferences. The relationship between a contractible space and a convex space was pointed out. Clearly, not all of the conditions discussed in this monograph have immediate intuitive appeal but, undoubtedly, they all fascinate through the intellectual sharpness and finesse which they manifest.

REFERENCES

Allen, B. 1996. 'A Remark on a Social Choice Problem', *Social Choice and Welfare*, 13: 11–16

Armstrong, W. E. 1951. 'Utility and the Theory of Welfare', *Oxford Economic Papers*, 3: 259–71

Arrow, K. J. 1950. 'A Difficulty in the Concept of Social Welfare', *The Journal of Political Economy*, 58: 328–46
1951, 1963. *Social Choice and Individual Values*, 2nd edn., 1963, New York: Wiley

Arrow, K. J. and Raynaud, H. 1986. *Social Choice and Multicriterion Decision-Making*, Cambridge, MA: MIT Press

Aumann, G. 1943. 'Über Räume mit Mittelbildungen', *Mathematische Annalen*, 119: 210–15

Baigent, N. 1987. 'Preference Proximity and Anonymous Social Choice', *Quarterly Journal of Economics*, 102: 161–9
1997. 'Discussion of Chichilnisky's Paper', in K. J. Arrow, A. Sen and K. Suzumura (eds.), *Social Choice Re-Examined*, 1, London: Macmillan

Baigent, N. and Huang, P. 1990. 'Topological Social Choice: Reply to Le Breton and Uriarte', *Social Choice and Welfare*, 7: 141–6

Baker, K. M. 1975. *Condorcet. From Natural Philosophy to Social Mathematics*, University of Chicago Press

Barberà, S., Massò, J. and Neme, A. 1999. 'Maximal Domains of Preferences Preserving Strategy-Proofness for Generalized Median Voter Schemes', *Social Choice and Welfare*, 16: 321–36

Barberà, S., Sonnenschein, H. and Zhou, L. 1991. 'Voting by Committees', *Econometrica*, 59: 595–609

Baryshnikov, Y. M. 1993. 'Unifying Impossibility Theorems: A Topological Approach', *Advances in Applied Mathematics*, 14: 404–15

References

1997. 'Topological and Discrete Social Choice: In Search of a Theory', *Social Choice and Welfare*, 14: 199–209

Batra, R. N. and Pattanaik, P. K. 1971. 'Transitivity of Social Decisions Under Some More General Group Decision Rules than the Method of Majority Decision', *The Review of Economic Studies*, 38: 295–304

1972a. 'Transitive Multi-Stage Majority Decisions with Quasi-Transitive Individual Preferences', *Econometrica*, 40: 1121–35

1972b. 'On Some Suggestions for Having Non-Binary Social Choice Functions', *Theory and Decision*, 3: 1–11.

Black, D. 1948. 'On the Rationale of Group Decision Making', *The Journal of Political Economy*, 56: 23–34

1958. *The Theory of Committees and Elections*, Cambridge University Press

Blair, D. and Muller, E. 1983. 'Essential Aggregation Procedures on Restricted Domains of Preferences', *Journal of Economic Theory*, 30: 34–53

Blau, J. H. 1957. 'Social Choice Functions and Simple Games', *Bulletin of the American Mathematical Society*, 57: 243–4

Blin, J.-M. and Satterthwaite, M. A. 1976. 'Strategy-Proofness and Single-Peakedness', *Public Choice*, 26: 51–8

1978. 'Individual Decisions and Group Decisions: The Fundamental Differences', *Journal of Public Economics*, 10: 247–67

Bloomfield, S. D. 1971. 'An Axiomatic Formulation of Constitutional Games', *Technical Report, no. 71–18*, Stanford University, Department of Operations Research

1976. 'A Social Choice Interpretation of the von Neumann–Morgenstern Game', *Econometrica*, 44: 105–14

Bloomfield, S. D. and Wilson, R. B. 1972. 'The Postulates of Game Theory', *The Journal of Mathematical Sociology*, 2: 221–34

Boadway, R. W. and Bruce, N. 1984. *Welfare Economics*, Oxford: Basil Blackwell

Borda, J. C. de 1781. *Mémoire sur les élections au scrutin*, Histoire de l'Académie Royale des Sciences, pp. 657–65

Border, K. 1983. 'Social Welfare Functions for Economic Environments with and without the Pareto Principle', *Journal of Economic Theory*, 29: 205–16

Bordes, G. and Le Breton, M. 1989. 'Arrovian Theorems with Private Alternatives Domains and Selfish Individuals', *Journal of Economic Theory*, 47: 257–81

References

1990. 'Arrovian Theorems for Economic Domains: The Case where there are Simultaneously Private and Public Goods', *Social Choice and Welfare*, 7: 1–17

Bowman, V. J. and Colantoni, C. S. 1972. 'The Extended Condorcet Condition: A Necessary and Sufficient Condition for the Transitivity of Majority Decision', *The Journal of Mathematical Sociology*, 2: 267–83

1973. 'Majority Rule under Transitivity Constraints', *Management Science*, 19: 1029–41

1974. 'Transitive Majority Rule and the Theorem of the Alternative', *Operations Research*, 32: 488–96

Campbell, D. E. 1990. 'Arrow's Theorem for Economic Environments and Effective Social Preferences', *Social Choice and Welfare*, 7: 325–9

1992. *Equity, Efficiency, and Social Choice*, Oxford: Clarendon Press

Campbell, D. E. and Kelly, J. S. 2000. 'A Simple Characterization of Majority Rule', *Economic Theory*, 15: 689–700

Chichilnisky, G. 1980. 'Social Choice and the Topology of Spaces of Preferences', *Advances in Mathematics*, 37: 165–76

1982a. 'Social Aggregation Rules and Continuity', *Quarterly Journal of Economics*, 97: 337–52

1982b. 'Structural Instability of Decisive Majority Rules', *Journal of Mathematical Economics*, 9: 207–21

1983. 'Social Choice and Game Theory: Recent Results with a Topological Approach', ch. 6 in P. K. Pattanaik and M. Salles (eds.), *Social Choice and Welfare*, Amsterdam: North-Holland

1991. 'Social Choice and the Closed Convergence Topology', *Social Choice and Welfare*, 8: 307–17

1993. 'On Strategic Control', *Quarterly Journal of Economics*, 108: 285–90

1994. 'Social Diversity, Arbitrage, and Gains from Trade: A Unified Perspective on Resource Allocation', *AEA Papers and Proceedings*, 84: 427–34

1995. 'Limited Arbitrage is Necessary and Sufficient for the Existence of a Competitive Equilibrium with or without Short Sales', *Economic Theory*, 5: 79–107

1996. 'A Robust Theory of Resource Allocation', *Social Choice and Welfare*, 13: 1–10

1997a. 'Market Arbitrage, Social Choice and the Core', *Social Choice and Welfare*, 14: 161–98

References

1997b. 'Limited Arbitrage is Necessary and Sufficient for the Existence of an Equilibrium', *Journal of Mathematical Economics*, 28: 470–9

1997c. 'A Unified Perspective on Resource Allocation: Limited Arbitrage is Necessary and Sufficient for the Existence of a Competitive Equilibrium, the Core and Social Choice', ch. 6 in K. J. Arrow, A. Sen and K. Suzumura (eds.), *Social Choice Re-Examined*, 1, London: Macmillan

Chichilnisky, G. and Heal, G. 1983. 'Necessary and Sufficient Conditions for a Resolution of the Social Choice Paradox', *Journal of Economic Theory*, 31: 68–87

1997. 'The Geometry of Implementation: A Necessary and Sufficient Condition for Straightforward Games', *Social Choice and Welfare*, 14: 259–94

Ching, S. 1994. 'An Alternative Characterization of the Uniform Rule', *Social Choice and Welfare*, 11: 131–6

Ching, S. and Serizawa, S. 1998. 'A Maximal Domain for the Existence of Strategy-Proof Rules', *Journal of Economic Theory*, 78: 157–66

Condorcet, Marquis de 1785. *Essai sur l'application de l'analyse à la probabilité des décisions rendues à la pluralité des voix*, Paris

Coombs, C. H. 1954. 'Social Choice and Strength of Preference', ch. VI in R. M. Thrall, C. H. Coombs and R. L. Davis (eds.), *Decision Processes*, New York: Wiley

1964. *A Theory of Data*, New York: Wiley

Cusanus, N. 1434. 'De Concordantia catholica', in G. Kallen (ed.), *Nicolai de Cusa Opera Omnia*, XIV, Hamburg: Felix Meiner

Dasgupta, P. and Maskin, E. 1998. 'On the Robustness of Majority Rule', *Discussion Paper*, Department of Economics, Harvard University, Cambridge, MA

D'Aspremont, C. and Gevers, L. 1977. 'Equity and the Informational Basis of Collective Choice', *Review of Economic Studies*, 46: 199–210

Debreu, G. 1952. 'A Social Equilibrium Existence Theorem', *Proceedings of the National Academy of Sciences of the United States of America*, 38: 886–93

De Marchi, N. 1987. 'Paradoxes and Anomalies', in J. Eatwell, M. Milgate, and P. Newman (eds.), *The New Palgrave*, London: Macmillan

Dodgson, C. L. [Lewis Carroll] 1876. *A Method of Taking Votes on More than Two Issues*, Oxford: Clarendon Press

References

Dummett, M. and Farquharson, R. 1961. 'Stability in Voting', *Econometrica*, 29: 33–43

Dutta, B. 1977. 'Existence of Stable Situations, Restricted Preferences and Strategic Manipulation under Democratic Group Decision Rules', *Journal of Economic Theory*, 15: 99–111

— 1980. 'On the Possibility of Consistent Voting Procedures', *The Review of Economic Studies*, 47: 603–16

Eckmann, B. 1954. 'Räume mit Mittelbildungen', *Commentarii mathematici Helvetici*, 28: 329–40

Eckmann, B., Ganea, T. and Hilton, P. J. 1962. *Generalized Means, Studies in Mathematical Analysis and Related Topics*, Stanford University Press

Farquharson, R. 1969. *Theory of Voting*, New Haven: Yale University Press

Feld, S. L. and Grofman, B. 1986. 'Partial Single-Peakedness: An Extension and Clarification', *Public Choice*, 51: 71–80

— 1987. 'Ideological Consistency as a Collective Phenomenon', *Discussion Paper*, School of Social Sciences, University of California, Irvine

Fine, K. 1972. 'Some Necessary and Sufficient Conditions for Representative Decisions on Two Alternatives', *Econometrica*, 40: 1083–90

— 1973. 'Conditions for the Existence of Cycles under Majority and Non-Minority Rules', *Econometrica*, 41: 889–99

Fishburn, P. C. 1970. 'Conditions for Simple Majority Decision Functions with Intransitive Individual Indifference', *Journal of Economic Theory*, 2: 354–67

— 1971. 'The Theory of Representative Majority Decision', *Econometrica*, 39: 273–84

— 1972a. 'A Location Theorem for Single-Peaked Preferences', *Journal of Economic Theory*, 4: 94–7

— 1972b. 'Conditions on Preferences that Guarantee a Simple Majority Winner', *The Journal of Mathematical Sociology*, 2: 105–12

— 1973. *The Theory of Social Choice*, Princeton University Press

— 1974. 'Social Choice Functions', *SIAM Review*, 16: 63–90

— 1975. 'Three-Valued Representative Systems', *Mathematical Systems Theory*, 9: 265–80

— 1979. 'Heights of Representative Systems', *Discrete Applied Mathematics*, 1: 181–99

Fishburn, P. C. and Gehrlein, W. V. 1980. 'The Paradox of Voting. Effects of Individual Indifference and Intransitivity', *Journal of Public Economics*, 14: 83–94

References

Fishburn, P. C., Gehrlein, W. V. and Maskin, E. 1979. 'Condorcet Proportions and Kelly's Conjectures', *Discrete Applied Mathematics*, 1: 229–52

Foley, D. 1967. 'Resource Allocation and the Public Sector', *Yale Economic Essays*, 7: 45–98

Gaertner, W. 1977. 'Zum Problem der Existenz von Sozialen Wohlfahrtsfunktionen im Sinne von Arrow', *Zeitschrift für die gesamte Staatswissenschaft*, 133: 61–74

1979. 'An Analysis and Comparison of Several Necessary and Sufficient Conditions for Transitivity under the Majority Decision Rule', in J.-J. Laffont (ed.), *Aggregation and Revelation of Preferences*, Amsterdam: North-Holland

1988. 'Binary Inversions and Transitive Majorities', in W. Eichhorn (ed.), *Measurement in Economics*, Heidelberg: Physica

Gaertner, W. and Heinecke, A. 1977. 'On Two Sufficient Conditions for Transitivity of the Social Preference Relation', *Zeitschrift für Nationalökonomie*, 37: 61–6

1978. 'Cyclically Mixed Preferences. A Necessary and Sufficient Condition for Transitivity of the Social Preference Relation', in H. W. Gottinger and W. Leinfellner (eds.), *Decision Theory and Social Ethics*, Dordrecht: Reidel

Gaertner, W. and Salles, M. 1981. 'Procédures d'agrégation avec domaines restreints et théorèmes d'existence', in P. Batteau, E. Jacquet-Lagrèze and B. Monjardet (eds.), *Analyse et agrégation des préférences*, Paris: Economica

Gale, D. 1960. *The Theory of Linear Economic Models*, New York: McGraw-Hill

Gans, J. S. and Smart, M. 1996. 'Majority Voting with Single-Crossing Preferences', *Journal of Public Economics*, 59: 219–37

Garman, M. and Kamien, M. 1968. 'The Paradox of Voting: Probability Calculations', *Behavioral Science*, 13: 306–16

Gehrlein, W. V. 1983. 'Condorcet's Paradox', *Theory and Decision*, 15: 161–97

1990. 'Probability Calculations for Transitivity of Simple Majority Rule with Anonymous Voters', *Public Choice*, 66: 253–9

1994. 'The Expected Likelihood of Transitivity: A Survey', *Theory and Decision*, 37: 175–209

References

1998a. 'Approximating the Probability that a Condorcet Winner Exists', *Discussion Paper*, University of Delaware, Department of Business Administration

1998b. 'The Probability of a Condorcet Winner with a Small Number of Voters', *Economics Letters*, 59: 317–21

Gehrlein, W. V. and Fishburn, P. C. 1976. 'The Probability of the Paradox of Voting: A Computable Solution', *Journal of Economic Theory*, 13: 14–25

1979. 'Proportions of Profiles with a Majority Candidate', *Computers and Mathematics with Applications*, 5: 117–24

Gibbard, A. 1973. 'Manipulation of Voting Schemes: A General Result', *Econometrica*, 41: 587–602

Gillett, R. 1978. 'A Recursion Relation for the Probability of the Paradox of Voting', *Journal of Economic Theory*, 18: 318–27

Graaff, J. de V. 1962. 'On Making a Recommendation in a Democracy', *Economic Journal*, 72: 293–300

1965. 'Notes on the Probability of Cyclical Majorities', Churchill College, Cambridge, unpublished

1967. *Theoretical Welfare Economics*, Cambridge University Press

Grandmont, J. M. 1978. 'Intermediate Preferences and the Majority Rule', *Econometrica*, 46: 317–30

Guilbaud, G. Th. 1952. 'Les théories de l'interêt général et le problème logique de l'agrégation', *Economie Appliquée*, 15: 502–84

Hamada, K. 1973. 'A Simple Majority Rule on the Distribution of Income', *Journal of Economic Theory*, 6, 243–64

Hansson, B. 1973. 'The Independence Condition in the Theory of Social Choice', *Theory and Decision*, 4: 25–49

Harsanyi, J. C. 1955. 'Cardinal Welfare, Individualistic Ethics, and Interpersonal Comparisons of Utility', *The Journal of Political Economy*, 63: 309–21

Heal, G. 1983. 'Contractibility and Public Decision-Making', ch. 7 in P. K. Pattanaik and M. Salles (eds.), *Social Choice and Welfare*, Amsterdam, North-Holland

1997. 'Social Choice and Resource Allocation: A Topological Perspective', *Social Choice and Welfare*, 14: 147–60

Hildenbrand, W. 1974. *Core and Equilibria of a Large Economy*, Princeton University Press

Honecker, M. 1937. 'Lullus-Handschriften aus dem Besitz des Kardinals Nikolaus von Cues: nebst einer Beschreibung der Lullus-Texte in Trier und einem Anhang über den wiedergefundenen Traktat "De Arte Eleccionis"', in H.

137

References

Finke (ed.), *Gesammelte Aufsätze zur Kulturgeschichte Spaniens*, Reihe I, Band 6, Münster in Westfalen: Verlag der Aschendorffschen Verlagsbuchhandlung

Horvath, Ch. D. 2001. 'On the Topological Social Choice Problem', Département de Mathématiques, Université de Perpignan, manuscript; *Social Choice and Welfare*, 18: 227–50

1996. 'Some Aspects of the Mathematical Background of the Topological Social Choice Problem', preliminary version, Département de Mathématiques, Université de Perpignan, manuscript

Hosomatsu, Y. 1978. 'Zero-Sum Condition: A Necessary and Sufficient Condition for a Transitive Voting System', *Journal of Economic Theory*, 18: 294–300

Inada, K. I. 1964a. 'On the Economic Welfare Function', *Econometrica*, 32: 316–38

1964b. 'A Note on the Simple Majority Decision Rule', *Econometrica*, 32: 525–31

1969. 'The Simple Majority Decision Rule', *Econometrica*, 37: 490–506

1970. 'Majority Rule and Rationality', *Journal of Economic Theory*, 2: 27–40

Jain, S. K. 1983. 'Necessary and Sufficient Conditions for Quasi-Transitivity and Transitivity of Special Majority Rules', *Keio Economic Studies*, 20: 55–63

1986a. 'Special Majority Rules. Necessary and Sufficient Condition for Quasi-Transitivity with Quasi-Transitive Individual Preferences', *Social Choice and Welfare*, 3: 99–106

1986b. 'Semi-Strict Majority Rules: Necessary and Sufficient Conditions for Quasi-Transitivity and Transitivity', Jawaharlal Nehru University, Centre for Economic Studies and Planning, New Delhi, unpublished

1987. 'Non-Minority Rules: Necessary and Sufficient Conditions for Quasi-Transitivity with Quasi-Transitive Individual Preferences', Jawaharlal Nehru University, Centre for Economic Studies and Planning, New Delhi, unpublished

Kalai, E. and Muller, E. 1977. 'Characterization of Domains Admitting Nondictatorial Social Welfare Functions and Nonmanipulable Voting Procedure', *Journal of Economic Theory*, 16: 457–69

Kalai, E., Muller, E. and Satterthwaite, M. A. 1979. 'Social Welfare Functions when Preferences are Convex, Strictly Monotonic, and Continuous', *Public Choice*, 34: 87–97

References

Kalai, E. and Ritz, Z. 1978. 'An Extended Single Peak Condition in Social Choice', *Discussion Paper*, 325, Graduate School of Management, Northwestern University

1980. 'Characterization of Private Alternatives Domains Admitting Arrow Social Welfare Functions', *Journal of Economic Theory*, 22: 23–36

Kaneko, M. 1975. 'Necessary and Sufficient Conditions for Transitivity in Voting Theory', *Journal of Economic Theory*, 11: 385–93

Kannai, Y. 1970. 'Continuity Properties of the Core of a Market', *Econometrica*, 38: 791–815

Kelly, J. S. 1974a. 'Necessity Conditions in Voting Theory', *Journal of Economic Theory*, 8: 149–60

1974b. 'Voting Anomalies, the Number of Voters, and the Number of Alternatives', *Econometrica*, 42: 239–51

1986. 'Condorcet Winner Proportions', in Section: Conjectures and Unsolved Problems, *Social Choice and Welfare*, 3: 311–14

1987. 'An Interview with Kenneth J. Arrow', *Social Choice and Welfare*, 4: 43–62

1991. 'Social Choice Bibliography', *Social Choice and Welfare*, 8:97–169 <http://www.maxwell.syr.edu./maxpages/faculty/jskelly/a.htm>

1994. 'The Bordes–Le Breton Exceptional Case', *Social Choice and Welfare*, 11: 273–81

Kemeny, J. G. and Snell, J. L. 1962. *Mathematical Models in the Social Sciences*, New York: Blaisdell

Kim, K. H. and Roush, F. W. 1980. *Introduction to Mathematical Consensus Theory*, New York: Dekker

1981. 'Effective Nondictatorial Domains', *Journal of Economic Theory*, 24: 40–7

Klaus, B. E. 1998. 'Fair Allocation and Reallocation: An Axiomatic Study', PhD thesis, Maastricht University

Kolm, S.-Ch. 1971. *Justice et équité*, Paris: CEPREMAP

Kramer, G. H. 1973. 'On a Class of Equilibrium Conditions for Majority Rule', *Econometrica*, 41: 285–97

Lagerspetz, E. 1986. 'Pufendorf on Collective Decisions', *Public Choice*, 49: 179–82

Le Breton, M. 1997. 'Arrovian Social Choice on Economic Domains', ch. 4 in K. J. Arrow, A. Sen and K. Suzumura (eds.), *Social Choice Re-Examined*, 1, London: Macmillan

References

Le Breton, M. and Uriarte, J. R. 1990a. 'On the Robustness of the Impossibility Result in the Topological Approach to Social Choice', *Social Choice and Welfare*, 7: 131–40

  1990b. 'Topological Social Choice: A Rejoinder', *Social Choice and Welfare*, 7: 147–8

Le Breton, M. and Weymark, J. 1996. 'An Introduction to Arrovian Social Welfare Functions on Economic and Political Domains', in N. Schofield (ed.), *Collective Decision Making: Social Choice and Political Economy*, Dordrecht: Kluwer

  2000. 'Arrovian Social Choice Theory on Economic Domains', ch. 8 in K. J. Arrow, A. Sen and K. Suzumura (eds.), *Handbook of Social Choice and Welfare*, forthcoming

Leininger, W. 1993. 'The Fatal Vote: Berlin versus Bonn', *Finanzarchiv*, NF, 50: 1–20

Luce, R. D. and Raiffa, H. 1957. *Games and Decisions*, New York: Wiley

Majumdar, T. 1969. 'Sen's General Theorem on Transitivity of Majority Decisions – An Alternative Approach', in T. Majumdar (ed.), *Growth and Choice*, Calcutta: Oxford University Press

Marglin, S. A. 1995. 'Deconstructing Individualism: A Step Towards an Economics of Community', Harvard University, Department of Economics

Mas-Colell, A. and Sonnenschein, H. 1972. 'General Possibility Theorems for Group Decisions', *The Review of Economic Studies*, 39: 185–92

Maskin, E. 1975. 'Arrow Social Welfare Functions and Cheat-Proof Game Forms on Restricted Domains: The Two-Person Case', *Discussion Paper*, Harvard University and University of Cambridge

  1976. 'Social Welfare Functions on Restricted Domains', *Discussion Paper*, Harvard University and Darwin College, Cambridge

  1995. 'Majority Rule, Social Welfare Functions, and Game Forms', in K. Basu, P. K. Pattanaik and K. Suzumura (eds.), *Choice, Welfare and Development. Festschrift for Amartya Sen*, Oxford: Clarendon Press

May, K. O. 1952. 'A Set of Independent Necessary and Sufficient Conditions for Simple Majority Decision', *Econometrica*, 20: 680–4

References

McKelvey, R. 1979. 'General Conditions for Global Intransitivities in Formal Voting Models', *Econometrica*, 47: 1085–1111

McLean, I. and London, J. 1990. 'The Borda and Condorcet Principles: Three Medieval Applications', *Social Choice and Welfare*, 7: 99–108

Monjardet, B. 1969. 'Remarques sur une classe de procédures de votes et les théorèmes de possibilité', in *La Décision*, Paris: Editions du CNRS

1978. 'An Axiomatic Theory of Tournament Aggregation', *Mathematics of Operations Research*, 3, 334–51

Monteiro, P. K., Page, F. H. and Wooders, M. H. 1997. 'Arbitrage, Equilibrium, and Gains from Trade: A Counterexample', *Journal of Mathematical Economics*, 28: 481–501

1999. 'Arbitrage and Global Cones: Another Counterexample', *Social Choice and Welfare*, 16: 337–46

Moulin, H. 1980. 'On Strategy-Proofness and Single-Peakedness', *Public Choice*, 35: 437–55

1988. 'Axioms of Cooperative Decision Making', *Econometric Society Monograph*, 15, Cambridge University Press

1996. 'Procedural cum Endstate Justice: An Implementation Viewpoint', Duke University, manuscript

Muller, E. and Satterthwaite, M. A. 1985. 'Strategy-Proofness: The Existence of Dominant-Strategy Mechanisms', in L. Hurwicz, D. Schmeidler and H. Sonnenschein (eds.), *Social Goals and Social Organization. Essays in Memory of Elisha Pazner*, Cambridge University Press

Murakami, Y. 1966. 'Formal Structure of Majority Decision', *Econometrica*, 34: 709–18

1968. *Logic and Social Choice*, London: Routledge & Kegan Paul

Nakamura, K. 1975. 'The Core of a Simple Game with Ordinal Preferences', *International Journal of Game Theory*, 4: 95–104

Nash, J. F. 1951. 'Non-Cooperative Games', *Annals of Mathematics*, 54: 286–95

Neumann, J. von and Morgenstern, O. 1953. *Theory of Games and Economic Behavior*, 3rd edn., Princeton University Press

Nicholson, M. 1965. 'Conditions for the "Voting Paradox" in Committee Decisions', *Metroeconomica*, 17: 29–44

References

Niemi, R. G. and Weisberg, H. F. 1968. 'A Mathematical Solution for the Probability of the Paradox of Voting', *Behavioral Science*, 13: 317–23

Page, F. H. and Wooders, M. H. 1994. 'Arbitrage in Markets with Unbounded Short Sales: Necessary and Sufficient Conditions for Nonemptiness of the Core and Existence of Equilibrium', *Department of Economics Working Paper*, 9409, University of Toronto

Pattanaik, P. K. 1970a. 'On Social Choice with Quasi-Transitive Individual Preferences', *Journal of Economic Theory*, 2: 267–75

1970b. 'Sufficient Conditions for the Existence of a Choice Set Under Majority Voting', *Econometrica*, 38: 165–70

1971. *Voting and Collective Choice*, Cambridge University Press

1973. 'On the Stability of Sincere Voting Situations', *Journal of Economic Theory*, 6: 558–74

1976. 'Collective Rationality and Strategy – Proofness of Group Decision Rules', *Theory and Decision*, 7: 191–203

1978. *Strategy and Group Choice*, Amsterdam: North-Holland

Pattanaik, P. K. and Sengupta, M. 1974. 'Conditions for Transitive and Quasi-Transitive Majority Decisions', *Economica*, 41: 414–23

Peleg, B. 1978. 'Representations of Simple Games by Social Choice Functions', *International Journal of Game Theory*, 7: 81–94

1984. *Game Theoretic Analysis of Voting in Committees*, Cambridge University Press

Pufendorf, S. 1688. *De jure naturae et gentium*, 2, trans. by C. H. and W. A. Oldfather, Oxford: Clarendon Press, 1934

Radice, B. 1969. *Pliny the Younger*, Letters and Panegyricus, I, Cambridge, MA: Harvard University Press

Rawls, J. 1971. *A Theory of Justice*, Cambridge, MA: Harvard University Press

Redekop, J. 1991. 'Social Welfare Functions on Restricted Economic Domains', *Journal of Economic Theory*, 53: 396–427

1993. 'Arrow-Inconsistent Economic Domains', *Social Choice and Welfare*, 10: 107–26

1996. 'Arrow Theorems in Mixed Goods, Stochastic, and Dynamic Environments', *Social Choice and Welfare*, 13: 95–112

References

Riker, W. H. 1958. 'The Paradox of Voting and Congressional Rules for Voting on Amendments', *American Political Science Review*, 52: 349–66

1986. 'The First Power Index', *Social Choice and Welfare*, 3: 293–5

Riker, W. H. and Ordeshook, P. C. 1973. *An Introduction to Positive Political Theory*, Englewood Cliffs, NJ: Prentice-Hall

Ritz, Z. 1983. 'Restricted Domains, Arrow Social Welfare Functions and Noncorruptible and Nonmanipulable Social Choice Correspondences: The Case of Private Alternatives', *Mathematical Social Sciences*, 4: 155–79

1985. 'Restricted Domains, Arrow Social Welfare Functions and Noncorruptible and Nonmanipulable Social Choice Correspondences: The Case of Private and Public Alternatives', *Journal of Economic Theory*, 35: 1–18

Roberts, K. W. S. 1977. 'Voting Over Income Tax Schedules', *Journal of Public Economics*, 8: 329–40

Romero, D. 1978. *Variations sur l'effet Condorcet. Thèse du troisième cycle*, Université de Grenoble

Rothstein, P. 1990. 'Order Restricted Preferences and Majority Rule', *Social Choice and Welfare*, 7: 331–42

Salles, M. 1974. 'A Note on Ken-Ichi Inada's "Majority Rule and Rationality"', *Journal of Economic Theory*, 8: 539–40

1975. 'A General Possibility Theorem for Group Decision Rules with Pareto-Transitivity', *Journal of Economic Theory*, 11: 110–18

1976. 'Characterization of Transitive Individual Preferences for Quasi-Transitive Collective Preference under Simple Games', *International Economic Review*, 17: 308–18

Saposnik, R. 1975a. 'Social Choice with Continuous Expression of Individual Preferences', *Econometrica*, 43: 683–90

1975b. 'On Transitivity of the Social Preference Relation under Simple Majority Rule', *Journal of Economic Theory*, 10: 1–7

n.d. 'A Necessary and Sufficient Condition for Transitivity of the Social Preference Relation under Simple Majority Rule', Georgia State University, Department of Economics

Satterthwaite, M. A. 1973. 'Existence of a Strategy-Proof Voting Procedure: A Topic in Social Theory', PhD dissertation, University of Wisconsin

1975. 'Strategy-Proofness and Arrow's Conditions: Existence and Correspondence Theorems for Voting Procedures and

References

Social Welfare Functions', *Journal of Economic Theory*, 10: 187–217

Schmeidler, D. and Sonnenschein, H. 1978. 'Two Proofs of the Gibbard–Satterthwaite Theorem on the Possibility of a Strategy-Proof Social Choice Function', in H. W. Gottinger and W. Leinfellner (eds.), *Decision Theory and Social Ethics*, Dordrecht: Reidel, pp. 227–34

Schofield, N. 1978. 'Instability of Simple Dynamic Games', *Review of Economic Studies*, 45: 575–94

Sen, A. K. 1966. 'A Possibility Theorem on Majority Decisions', *Econometrica*, 34: 491–9

1970. *Collective Choice and Social Welfare*, San Francisco: Holden-Day

1985. 'Social Choice and Justice: A Review Article', *Journal of Economic Literature*, 23: 1764–76

1986. 'Social Choice Theory', in K. J. Arrow and M. D. Intriligator (eds.), *Handbook of Mathematical Economics*, III, Amsterdam: North-Holland, pp. 1073–1181

1987. 'Social Choice', in J. Eatwell, M. Milgate and P. Newman (eds.), *The New Palgrave*, London: Macmillan

Sen, A. K. and Pattanaik, P. K. 1969. 'Necessary and Sufficient Conditions for Rational Choice under Majority Decision', *Journal of Economic Theory*, 1: 178–202

Sengupta, M. and Dutta, B. 1979. 'A Condition for Nash-Stability under Binary and Democratic Group Decision Functions', *Theory and Decision*, 10: 293–309

Serizawa, S. 1995. 'Power of Voters and Domain of Preferences Where Voting by Committees is Strategy-Proof', *Journal of Economic Theory*, 67: 599–608

Shapley, L. 1962. 'Simple Games: An Outline of the Descriptive Theory', *Behavioral Science*, 7: 59–66

Shepsle, K. A. and Weingast, B. R. 1982. 'Institutionalizing Majority Rule: A Social Choice Theory with Policy Implications', *American Economic Review, Papers and Proceedings*, 72: 367–71

Shubik, M. 1959. *Strategy and Market Structure*, New York: Wiley

Slutsky, S. 1975. 'Majority Voting and the Allocation of Public Goods', PhD dissertation, Yale University

1977. 'A Characterization of Societies with Consistent Majority Decision', *The Review of Economic Studies*, 44: 211–25

References

Sprumont, Y. 1991. 'The Division Problem with Single-Peaked Preferences: A Characterization of the Uniform Allocation Rule', *Econometrica*, 59: 509–19

Steiner, H. 1994. *An Essay on Rights*, Oxford: Blackwell

Thomson, W. 1994. 'Consistent Solutions to the Problem of Fair Division when Preferences are Single-Peaked', *Journal of Economic Theory*, 63: 219–45

—— 1998. 'The Theory of Fair Allocation', Princeton University Press, forthcoming

Tucker, A. W. 1956. 'Dual Systems of Homogeneous Linear Relations', in H. W. Kuhn and A. W. Tucker (eds.), *Linear Inequalities and Related Systems*, Princeton University Press

Tullock, G. 1967. 'The General Irrelevance of the General Impossibility Theorem', *Quarterly Journal of Economics*, 81: 256–70

—— 2000. 'Why No Cycles', *Atlantic Economic Journal*, 28: 1–13

Vickrey, W. 1960. 'Utility, Strategy and Social Decision Rules', *Quarterly Journal of Economics*, 74: 507–35

Ward, B. 1965. 'Majority Voting and Alternative Forms of Public Enterprises', in J. Margolis (ed.), *The Public Economy of Urban Expenditures*, Baltimore: Johns Hopkins University Press, pp. 112–26

Weingast, B. R. 1995. 'Self-Enforcing Democracy: Its Maintenance and Collapse in Antebellum America', Hoover Institution and Stanford University, Department of Political Science, manuscript

Weinstein, A. A. 1968. 'Individual Preference Intransitivity', *Southern Economic Journal*, 34: 335–43

Williamson, O. E. and Sargent, T. J. 1967. 'Social Choice: A Probabilistic Approach', *Economic Journal*, 77: 797–813

Wilson, R. B. 1972. 'The Game-Theoretic Structure of Arrow's General Possibility Theorem', *Journal of Economic Theory*, 5: 14–20

Zeckhauser, R. 1973. 'Voting Systems, Honest Preferences and Pareto Optimality', *The American Political Science Review*, 67: 934–46

AUTHOR INDEX

Author index

Author index

SUBJECT INDEX

149

Subject index

maximal domain, 66, 68
maximin rule, 72
means, 108, 112
median voter, 69, 94
metric, 117
monotonicity, 32, 39, 55, 71, 100,
    101, 115, 116, 127, 128
multi-dimensional choice space,
    8, 99
multi-stage majority decision
    rule, 31–34

neutrality, 63, 67, 71
non-minority decision, 27, 42
nondictatorial decomposability,
    51, 59, 62
nondictatorship, 13, 15, 49, 50,
    60, 62, 103, 123
nonempty choice set, 5, 23, 42
nonmanipulable
    game, 113
    voting procedure, 13, 46, 58–60,
        62, 66
nontrivial
    decomposition, 57, 58
    pair, 47, 48, 50–54
not-strictly-best value restriction,
    41, 42, 85, 86
not-strictly-medium value
    restriction, 41
not-strictly-worst value
    restriction, 41, 42, 85, 86

oddness requirement, 21, 22, 33,
    34
order restriction, 23

pairwise comparison, 2
paradox of voting, 1, 34
parafinite CW complex, 107, 111,
    112
Pareto
    condition, 47, 50, 59, 60, 64, 65,
        103, 105
    extension rule, 65
partial agreement, 28, 30, 95

party structure, 7
pivotal voter, 102
plurality rule, 3
polyhedra, 107, 112
positive responsiveness, 63, 64
preference
    proximity, 88
    vector, 96
price mechanism, 121, 124
private
    component, 55
    good, 52, 54, 55, 100
probability
    distribution, 80–82
    of a majority cycle, 35
proper simple game, 40, 41, 43
proximity, 88, 91, 103, 117
public
    component, 55
    goods, 8, 48, 50, 52, 55, 99, 128
    opinion, 119

quasi-agreement, 65, 66
quasi-concavity, 8
quasi-transitivity, 5, 11, 12, 17,
    22, 24–31, 34, 44, 45, 76, 83,
    93, 94, 97, 98

range, 5, 13, 14, 18, 26, 44, 69, 114
rank-order method, 2, 3, 96
real line, 8, 82, 106, 113
reduced
    preference profile, 7, 88, 89, 91
    set, 83, 93
reduction procedure, 83, 89, 90
representative system, 32
resoluteness, 72, 74
restricted Pareto optimality, 73
retraction, 107, 108, 111, 112
robustness, 63–66

saturating domain, 48, 49, 52, 55
secret voting, 3
selfish preference, 52, 53, 56
semi-strict majority rule, 27–29
separability, 67
separation condition, 54

Subject index